"*You Are M̶̶̶̶̶̶ ̶̶̶̶̶̶̶ ̶̶̶̶ ̶̶̶̶ Gold* captures the soul and speaks life to the young at heart. It is more than just a book—it is the pathway to a deeper relationship with God."

Captain Terry Masango of The Salvation Army

"*You Are More Precious Than Gold* will help teenage girls understand who God has created them to be. Sarah's heart for leading people closer to Jesus is evident in her writing. This book will be helpful to any young woman who is seeking to understand her place in the world."

**Captain Jennifer Hale, Divisional Youth Secretary
for Ontario Great Lakes Division**

"Sarah has provided a practical tool to help young women look to the Word as their guide through all areas of life. The scriptures shared remind the reader that God has provided everything we need to live a godly life and a God-honouring life."

**Nancy Turley, Territorial Abuse Advisor,
The Salvation Army Canada and Bermuda Territory**

"Through scripture references and her own personal testimony, Sarah has been able to clearly and creatively express the true source of beauty that is found only in Christ. She is wise beyond her years in how she presents this truth. I know that this book will be of encouragement and enlightenment for many women as it has been for me."

**Glenda Davis, Area Commander for
The Salvation Army Ontario Great Lakes Division**

You Are More Precious Than Gold is aimed at young women, but it's inspiring to all ages. I read Sarah's book at a time when I was facing some challenges in my own ministry. Her words were a touching reminder that I am a daughter of the Most High God. We can find rest in His love and be energized in His plans. At the end of each chapter, Sarah offers several Scripture passages for meditation, while inviting us to ponder a specific truth. This book is practical, insightful, and challenging. Through her own vulnerability and honesty, Sarah invites us to see how great the love of Jesus is for all of us.

Major (Pastor) April McNeilly of The Salvation Army

You Are *More Precious* than *Gold*

Inspiring Young Women to Embrace their *Inner* Beauty

You Are *More Precious* than *Gold*

Sarah Evangeline

YOU ARE MORE PRECIOUS THAN GOLD
Copyright © 2017 by Sarah Evangeline
Back cover photo taken by Lisa Campbell

All rights reserved. Neither this publication nor any part of this publication may be reproduced or transmitted in any form or by any means, electronic or mechanical, including photocopying, recording or any information storage and retrieval system, without permission in writing from the author.

Unless otherwise indicated, all scripture quotations taken from the Holy Bible, NEW INTERNATIONAL VERSION®. Copyright © 1973, 1978, 1984, 2011 by Biblica, Inc. All rights reserved worldwide. Used by permission. NEW INTERNATIONAL VERSION® and NIV® are registered trademarks of Biblica, Inc. Use of either trademark for the offering of goods or services requires the prior written consent of Biblica US, Inc. • Scripture quotations marked (KJV) are taken from the Holy Bible, King James Version, which is in the public domain. • Scripture quotations marked (GNT) are taken from the Good News Translation® (Today's English Version, Second Edition), Copyright © 1992 American Bible Society. All rights reserved. Bible text from the Good News Translation (GNT) is not to be reproduced in copies or otherwise by any means except as permitted in writing by American Bible Society, 1865 Broadway, New York, NY 10023. • Scripture quotations marked (MSG) are taken from The Message. Copyright © by Eugene H. Peterson 1993, 1994, 1995, 1996, 2000, 2001, 2002. Used by permission of NavPress Publishing Group. • Scripture quotations marked (ESV) are taken from The Holy Bible, English Standard Version® (ESV®), copyright © 2001 by Crossway, a publishing ministry of Good News Publishers. Used by permission. All rights reserved. • Scripture quotations marked (NLT) are taken from the Holy Bible, New Living Translation, copyright ©1996, 2004, 2007 by Tyndale House Foundation. Used by permission of Tyndale House Publishers, Inc., Carol Stream, Illinois 60188. All rights reserved. • Scripture quotations marked (NKJV) are taken from the New King James Version®. Copyright © 1982 by Thomas Nelson, Inc. Used by permission. All rights reserved. • Scripture quotations marked (NASB) are taken from the New American Standard Bible®, Copyright ©1960, 1962, 1963, 1968, 1971, 1972, 1973, 1975, 1977, 1995 by The Lockman Foundation. Used by permission. • Scripture quotations marked (TLB) are taken from The Living Bible copyright © 1971 by Tyndale House Foundation. Used by permission of Tyndale House Publishers Inc., Carol Stream, Illinois 60188. All rights reserved. The Living Bible, TLB, and the The Living Bible logo are registered trademarks of Tyndale House Publishers.

Printed in Canada

ISBN: 978-1-4866-1404-2

Word Alive Press
131 Cordite Road, Winnipeg, MB R3W 1S1
www.wordalivepress.ca

Library and Archives Canada Cataloguing in Publication
Evangeline, Sarah, author
    You are more precious than gold : inspiring young women to embrace their inner beauty / Sarah Evangeline.

Issued in print and electronic formats.
ISBN 978-1-4866-1404-2 (paperback).--ISBN 978-1-4866-1405-9 (ebook)

    1. Young women--Religious life. 2. Christian women--Religious life.
3. Beauty, Personal--Religious aspects--Christianity. I. Title.

BV4551.3.E83 2017   248.8'33   C2016-906494-8
                                             C2016-906495-6

dedication

TO THE TWO MOST BEAUTIFUL WOMEN IN MY LIFE—MY GRANDMOTHER, Ann, and my mother, Lynn. Thank you for being living examples of true inner beauty and for always showing me how to follow Christ.

Also to Devan, the twelve-year-old girl from Sudbury who reminded me what a joy it is to live for the Lord, and who inspired me to put my words onto paper.

contents

acknowledgements

SPECIAL THANKS TO MY DEAR FRIENDS, KATHRYN GROSS, CORISA Miller, Jordan Robinson, Rebecca Reimer, Emily Sears, Cassie Barrett, Rebekah McNeilly, Annalee Roffel, and Kelly Zuidema. Your words of wisdom and your love for Jesus have helped this book come to life. I pray and hope you all continue to live for Jesus, wherever He may take you.

Special thanks to Lisa Campbell Photography. Lisa, you are and forever will be my most loyal friend. Thank you for your encouragement, support, and laughter from beginning to end of this project. You have a true talent for photography.

Thank you to my family for always loving me, even at my worst. Your constant love and support helped inspire this book to come to life. Mom, you have been a living example of Christ in my life since I was a little girl. Your radiance of His beauty only gets stronger as time goes on. Thank you, thank you for everything you have done for me.

Thank you to all my church leaders, mentors, and other friends (you know who you are) who believed in me and spoke life into my life. Your words of kindness and grace helped motivate me to live out this dream and passion.

Most importantly, thank you, heavenly Father, for giving me these words. May Your name be glorified.

foreword
By: Commissioner Rosalie Peddle

MY NAME IS COMMISSIONER ROSALIE PEDDLE, AND I AM A SALVATION Army officer. My homeland is Canada, but I am presently serving with the Salvation Army at our International Headquarters in London, England. My appointment is the World Secretary for Women's Ministries. The Salvation Army works in 128 countries around the world, and I have the privilege of travelling to these countries to observe the various ministries that women are involved in as they reach out to communities with Christ-like compassion and love. These ministries include human trafficking, social justice issues, developing life skills, education classes, and women's leadership development. I have the opportunity to coach, speak, contribute, and learn as I travel. My aim is to encourage, inspire, motivate, and empower women to be who God has created them to be so that they will have a significant impact on their world for good and for God.

Christian young women desperately seek for a deeper meaning and purpose in their lives. They desire inspiration and insight that will lead them towards a solid, growing relationship with God. They aspire to embrace love, joy, peace, and a healthy balance to their lives. They crave to experience an emotionally, spiritually, and physically healthy life. They yearn for respect, approval, value, and acceptance. They long to experience friendships and relationships that are meaningful and lasting. They strive to be beautiful both inside and outside. Not always that easy! Life is not always that fair! The temptations and lures of the evil one can be strong and overpowering. There is hope! There is a way to overcome and be strong, because God has made us beautiful in His image and for His glory.

Sarah Evangeline is extremely courageous in intertwining her testimony, her life experiences, her faith, powerful Scripture, and God's incredible grace in this soul-captivating book that will speak deep into the hearts of young women who are trying to live out their God- given faith in a complicated world where evil is present.

You Are More Precious Than Gold will be an exceptional tool for young women in their personal growth, as well as for group Bible study or teaching purposes. The scriptural references and teachings throughout this book are rock solid truths and significantly relevant to the spiritual development of young women who are seeking God's will and purpose for their lives as they learn to love themselves as much as God loves them.

You Are More Precious Than Gold is an inspiring book that will open the spiritual eyes of young women to truly see their inner beauty as God has created them in His perfect eyes and boundless passion. The psalmist reminds us that we are fearfully and wonderfully made! God is the very essence of what makes us beautiful, and with His courage and grace, we can live our lives in freedom and peace. He created us for a purpose. He promised His presence with us at all times, and He desires to have a strong relationship with us. God will not forget you. He has written your name in the palms of His hands:

> *Can a mother forget the baby at her breast and have no compassion on the child she has borne? Though she may forget, I will not forget you! See, I have engraved you on the palms of my hands; your walls are ever before me.* (Isaiah 49:15–16)

Sarah Evangeline might be a young woman, but she writes with maturity, clarity, passion, skill, and conviction. *More Precious Than Gold* will set your heart aflame by the Holy Spirit as you realize how much you are loved by God. He created you and declares you are beautiful inside and out! God will use this book to inspire and motivate young women to fully embrace their lives as God has created them to be, and with great joy and the spirit of true beauty, they will impact and make a difference in their world. An inspiring book that needs to be placed in the hands of young women all around the world!

"Therefore we do not lose heart. Though outwardly [our outer beauty] *we are wasting away, yet inwardly* [our inner beauty] *we are being renewed day by day,"*
(2 Corinthians 4:16)

introduction

I AM SO EXCITED TO SHARE THIS BOOK WITH YOU. OVER THE COURSE of my walk with God, He has taught me so many things about what this life truly means and why we were all created. Along this journey, I have made many mistakes, wandered off the path, and spent so much time doubting God. Oh, but my God is everywhere, and He has brought me to a place where all I want to do is live for Him. He has taken me on this incredible adventure I call faith.

I've been taught to live for God and follow Him. But how can we expect to do this if we don't have the proper tools and teaching? If you and I don't understand the truth that our identity is found in Christ alone, we'll start to follow the world's definition of beauty, which is a long road to destruction.

Proverbs 3 is a passage that does not solely pertain to women, but it does present a deep reflection of God's love for us. Here is a paraphrase of Proverbs 3:13–18, the verses upon which I based this book:

Blessed is the woman who finds her wisdom and identity in Christ,
For her value is worth more than silver or jewels.
She is more precious than gold.
Her pathway is sure, good, and peaceful.
When others see her, no one can compare.
and nothing can compare with her.

She has a long, strong life ahead, for she is a tree of life.
But you see, with God, every woman is more precious than gold.

There will never be another girl who has your personality, your ambition, or your dreams. I think that's pretty amazing. Your outside appearance—your hair, your height, and even your skin colour—has been given to you. You have no control over those features, but the inside is up to you. I have learned time and time again that the inside always wins and exceeds the outside.

I started writing this book a few years ago, not knowing if it would be published or just put away in my drawer. *You Are More Precious Than Gold* is not just a book, but a pathway to fully understand that when we find our identity in God, He becomes our beauty mark.

God is the very essence of what makes us beautiful. God wants you to find your beauty through Him. God created you, chose you, and knows you are worth more than gold. This kind of wisdom and truth is all about inner beauty. It all starts with God and is woven into every aspect of our being. It grows deep into our soul and allows us to be radiant from the inside out. It affects all areas of our life and it never stops until we reach the gates of heaven.

I cannot promise you an easy and perfect life, but I can promise you that life with God is the best way to live. Some days I think the good Lord gave me way too much energy. God has given me a passion to write. There is a desire rooted deep in my soul to help inspire young women to find their identity in Him so that they can know the true meaning of beauty. I think I'll write for the rest of my life, as it releases so many truths that are wrapped up inside of me. I cannot stop until you hear this good news. I'm just an imperfect girl who loves a perfect and glorious King.

Will you join me in this journey? Will you allow God to change you from the inside out? I am asking you to allow God to become your beauty mark. I don't walk this road alone, because I believe in God. I hope you will experience the same joy and abundance of grace that comes from knowing that our beauty lies in our Creator.

Your sister in Christ,

Sarah Evangeline

chapter one

Created for So Much More than an Ordinary Life

Spread love [and Gold] *everywhere you go. Let no
one ever come to you without leaving happier.*[1]
MOTHER TERESA

EVERY TIME I PACK UP MY SUITCASE, HIT THE ROAD, AND FORGET ABOUT schedules and the "busy life," God takes the wheel to show me the wonders of His world in new and profound ways. This time I was headed to the beautiful mountains of Colorado. Wow, were they magnificent! No matter where I turned, there they were—so beautiful and full of power. A reminder of true strength. It was like the mountains were never ending as they soared up to kiss the heavens. As I stared at the grace and strength before me, I knew my God was more than anything this world could offer. It was here that I realized God created me for more than an ordinary life. I cannot stop until I share this truth with you.

That day, God gave me a new approach to how I should live my life. He reminded me that my sole purpose is not really my purpose, but *His purpose*. He is the reason I get out of bed in the morning. He is the reason I take the risks. He is the reason I must go where I don't really want to go. For God alone is my Father, my Saviour, my Refuge, and the King of my heart. He is how I embrace my true inner beauty to acquire all He has to offer me.

Have you ever felt so dirty and broken that you don't believe you deserve to be called beautiful? Does this world ever make you feel so unworthy? Do you ever feel so lonely that you can't find the strength to carry on? Or maybe you're already a Christian, but you're tired of just drifting through life. I'm guilty of all these feelings, but we don't have to live like this. God created us for so much more. You and I have the chance to bring this world back to how God first intended it to be—a chance to worship God as if it were natural and free, a chance to love others first rather than ourselves, and a chance to forgive, because that is what Christ did for us. This is your time to truly know and believe that we are made beautiful and whole in His sight. This only inspires me to keep on living. Ephesians 1:11 says:

> *It's in Christ that we find out who we are and what we are living for. Long before we first heard of Christ … he had his eye on us, had designs on us for a glorious living, part of the overall purpose he is working out in everything and everyone.* (MSG)

Acts 17:28 says, "*For in Him we live and move and have our being.*" Does this inspire you as much as it inspires me? You are created for so much more than an ordinary life.

No matter where you are today, no matter how you feel today, I encourage you to open up your mind and heart to the truth that God loves you. I hope and pray you start seeing yourself the way God sees you. This is not an easy, overnight, one-time decision. It's going to take surrender, obedience, and faith. This is also going to mean taking the time to build your relationship with God. Don't put the book down; as you keep reading, I'll share with you how you can move into completeness in Christ. Hold on to your seats, girls … you are in for the best ride of your life.

It's God's evident plan from the beginning of time to make our purpose *His purpose*. When we forget about ourselves and focus on the One who is the source of all life, living this crazy, messed up, dark, unpredictable life starts to make sense, and we begin to realize why we are truly meant to be here. God sees your pain. He sees your sleepless nights. He sees when people laugh and judge you. He sees you sitting in the back of the classroom, wishing the anxieties and depressive thoughts would leave your mind. He sees you when you look in the mirror and dislike what you see. He knows you more than anyone ever will. He is here, and He calls you to His glorious purpose. This is the secret to living.

I'm just an imperfect girl who loves a perfect God. I was just a scared and worried girl who became fearless in Christ. I was the girl who was empty and broken, but I found my worth and identity in my Lord and Saviour. I hope you'll start this journey with me, for when you find this truth and grace, you'll never want to stop living it out.

He is waiting for you. He is longing for you. He has chosen you. He adores you. I hope you're feeling the sweet joy deep in your soul. I hope you feel a sensation unlike anything this world can offer you. Yes, you will still have your bad days. Yes, you will still feel pain, but with God, you will become unshakable.

God holds the whole universe in His hands. He formed you in your mother's womb. He knew all your days before they even came to be. This is how big our Father and King is, and how much He adores and loves us. Throughout this book, I hope you start to realize the glorious grace and love God unleashes to us all.

You Are Golden

As women, it can be hard to believe and understand that God created us for more than anything this world offers us. It can be hard to get past all the lies of the world. Here are some lies that get in the way of the knowledge that we are created for more than an ordinary life.

Lie: Physical beauty matters more than inner beauty.

Truth: God tells us through His Word that inner beauty is far more important than outer beauty. Beauty lies within us: "*Therefore we do not lose heart. Though outwardly* [our outer beauty] *we are wasting away, yet inwardly* [our inner beauty] *we are being renewed day by day,*" (2 Corinthians 4:16).

Lie: Life is all about me. I can live it any way I want.

Truth: Sure, you can do what you want, but that means you're missing out on a life that's all about God and His purpose for your life.

Lie: I'm not worth anything.

Truth: Your value and worth are found in the way God views you, not in the world's definition of beauty. We are worth more than gold.

Lie: God's way cannot be my way.

Truth: God's ways are always best. God's ways are always good. God holds you in the palm of His hand. Surrender to Him, and you will start to see His desires becoming yours.

Lie: I can't change how messed up my life is right now.

Truth: God can change you from the inside out.

God wants us to be women after His own heart. Dear sisters, you are worth so much more than settling for what this world calls beautiful. You deserve to know that you are adorned by the King, the Creator of the universe, the One who knew you before you were born. You are His daughter and forever cherished by Him. It's time for you to believe that you are more precious than gold. Proverbs 31 is a description of this:

Who can find a virtuous and capable wife? She is more precious than rubies [gold] … She brings him good, not harm, all the days of her life … She gets up before dawn to prepare breakfast for her household … She is energetic and strong, a hard worker. She makes sure her dealings are profitable; her lamp burns late into the night … She extends a helping hand to the poor and opens her arms to the needy … She is clothed with strength and dignity, and she laughs without fear of the future. When she speaks, her words are wise, and she gives instructions with kindness. (Proverbs 31:10, 12, 15, 17–18, 20, 25–26)

You are golden. God has planted the true meaning of this beauty and wisdom inside of you. I believe embracing our inner beauty unlocks the way God intended us to live our life. True inner beauty doesn't fade with age; it will never outgrow us, because it lives inside of us, rooted deep in our soul, and eventually shining outwards. Inner beauty is accepting ourselves through all our good and bad qualities. Inner beauty is about learning to become Christ-like through compassion, kindness, love, strength, wisdom, and integrity. God is searching the world for people who can represent Him in this way: "*The eyes of the Lord search the whole earth in order to strengthen those whose hearts are fully committed to Him,*" (2 Chronicles 16:9, NLT).

This kind of living encompasses so much more than my little fingers can type at this moment. What joy is born when we live this way! Happiness is only what this world offers you, but joy is what God gives you when you live out life this way. Joy is grown deep inside your soul, and no one can take it away.

Do you want to discover the amazing grace that never ends? Through this journey, I will also share with you my own personal experiences and stories about how God has helped me embrace my inner beauty. I'm still a work in process, but I'm so grateful for where God has brought me. I hope I can inspire you today to start moving into greater completion in Christ. Psalm 46:5 says: "*God is within her, she will not fall; God will help her at break of day.*"

Before you read on, I must ask you to do something that is very important. Can you let go and let God take you into the unknown? Can you leave this world behind and run into the arms of Jesus? Being open to whatever the Lord may say or wherever He may take you is the best way to live. Embracing your inner beauty is all about the unknown. I don't know about you, but I want to be a woman who trusts God, even when I don't yet understand or know what is ahead. Remember, God will go before you, and you will never be alone: "*Those who look to Him are radiant; their faces are never covered with shame,*" (Psalm 34:5); "*He has made everything beautiful in its time,*" (Ecclesiastes 3:11a).

Do you know how precious you are? Do you realize what a gift you are to people around you? Do you know there is more to life than the world's definition of beauty? Let God change you from the inside out.

God Never Called Us to "Fit in"

Living an extraordinary life for God means we'll be different than the rest of the world. I define "extraordinary" as a woman who is remarkable, a woman who shines her light in the darkness. When you go into the unknown, when you start embracing all of who you are, you will be different from many of your friends and even some of your family. You will face times of suffering and pain because you choose a different path. You may experience loneliness and heartache because you are a follower of Christ, not a follower of the world. Even I, who have known God for a number of years, still experience times of suffering and pain because I love my God. Rick Warren gives us some encouragement from his book, *The Purpose Driven Life*:

> You will find that people who do not understand your shape for ministry will criticize you and try to get you to conform to what they think you should be doing. Ignore them. Paul the apostle had to deal with critics who misunderstood and maligned his service. His response was always the same: avoid comparisons, resist exaggerations and seek only God's commendation.[2]

I encourage you to focus less on what others think of you and rest in the truth of how much God treasures you.

Fearfully and Wonderfully Made

Psalm 139 is one of my favourite chapters from the Bible because it is a testimony of how much God loves us and has chosen us. As you read these words, ponder them and think deeply about how much God loves you and calls you to His purpose.

You have searched me, LORD, and you know me. You know when I sit and when I rise; you perceive my thoughts from afar. You discern my going out and my lying down; you are familiar with all my ways. Before a word is on my tongue you, LORD, know it completely. You hem me in behind and before, and you lay your hand upon me. Such knowledge is too wonderful for me, too lofty for me to attain. Where can I go from your Spirit?

Where can I flee from your presence? If I go up to the heavens, you are there; if I make my bed in the depths, you are there. If I rise on the wings of the dawn, if I settle on the far side of the sea, even there your hand will guide me, your right hand will hold me fast. If I say, "Surely the darkness will hide me and the light become night around me," even the darkness will not be dark to you; the night will shine like the day, for darkness is as light to you. For you created my inmost being; you knit me together in my mother's womb. I praise you because I am fearfully and wonderfully made; your works are wonderful, I know that full well. My frame was not hidden from you when I was made in the secret place, when I was woven together in the depths of the earth. Your eyes saw my unformed body; all the days ordained for me were written in your book before one of them came to be. How precious to me are your thoughts, God! How vast is the sum of them! Were I to count them, they would outnumber the grains of sand—when I awake, I am still with you ... Search me, God, and know my heart; test me and know my anxious thoughts. See if there is any offensive way in me, and lead me in the way everlasting.

Celebrate

It is a time to celebrate! Kick off your shoes, put on the music, and know that this life, the journey and adventure ahead, is a good one. As you read this passage from the book of Psalms, allow your mind, heart, and body to rejoice in celebration.

I will praise the Lord, who counsels me ... Therefore my heart is glad and my tongue rejoices; my body also will rest secure ...

you make known to me the path of life; you will fill me with joy in your presence, with eternal pleasures at your right hand. (Psalm 16:7,9,11)

I know that God is a God who celebrates. Once His daughters realize their purpose for living, there is a party in heaven. The best way to live is to join Him in this celebration: "... *I have hope: Because of the Lord's great love we are not consumed, for His compassions never fail. They are new every morning,*" (Lamentations 3:21–23). This world knows how to stop celebrating and forget about the hope of life, but you and I are on a road of rejoicing, honour, and celebration: "*I will celebrate before the Lord,*" (2 Samuel 6:21a).

Throughout this book, I hope you can celebrate the beauty God has given you. If you read my introduction, then you know that when you let God in, He becomes our beauty mark. He is the very essence of what makes us beautiful ... so celebrate!

Be Empowered

"Charm is deceitful, and beauty is vain, but a woman who fears the Lord is to be praised," (Proverbs 31:30, ESV).

"Those who look to him are radiant, and their faces shall never be ashamed," (Psalm 34:5, ESV).

"For we are his workmanship, created in Christ Jesus for good works, which God prepared beforehand, that we should walk in them," (Ephesians 2:10, ESV).

"Trust in the Lord with all your heart ... and He will make straight your paths," (Proverbs 3:6, ESV).

Thought to Ponder
To the Girl Who Is Searching for Purpose
By: Kelly Zuidema

When you woke up this morning, what was the first thing you did? Make breakfast? Read your Bible? Look in the mirror? I'm willing to bet that over 90 per cent of you went immediately to the mirror that hangs in your room. Please be assured that I don't say this to make you feel ashamed, as I am guilty of it too, but I want to make a point and pose this question: Is what we value really worth valuing? The Bible tells us that beauty is vain.

Surveys show that teenage girls spend thirty-one hours a week watching television, seventeen hours a week listening to music, three hours a week watching movies, four hours a week reading magazines, and ten hours a week online. That's almost eleven hours of media consumption a day. That's eleven hours every single day that you're being lied to about who you are, what you're here for, and just how deeply you're valued. Think about this—if we're spending this much time immersed in media that stands in direct opposition to our Christian paradigm, soon our spirits will start to feel conflicted. Just like tea turns bitter if steeped for a lengthy time, our spirits will be fundamentally changed by what we put into them.

Dear one, if it is truth you seek, if you're wondering who you were made to be and where to find your value, I plead with you to dedicate your mind and heart to seeing yourself as God sees you. He made you! I wish you could have been there to see Him smile on the day He stroked your hair into perfect place and chose the colour of your eyes. You are declared "very (exceedingly, completely, totally, perfectly) good" by the King of earth and heaven. He proclaims that you are "fearfully and wonderfully made." God is the only one who holds the truth about who you are. In order to enter into this truth, we must come to Jesus with humility. It's very hard for a heart filled with pride to understand how Jesus thinks and how His Kingdom works. Paul tells us:

It is in Christ that we find out who we are and what we are living for. Long before we first heard of Christ and got our hopes up, he had his eye on us, had designs for glorious living, part of the overall purpose he is working out in everything and everyone. (Ephesians 1:11–12, MSG)

This is one of the most important things about how God sees us: "*It is in Christ that we find out who we are and what we are living for.*" He created us in His image. This means that you and I are the reflections of Jesus here on the earth. A reflection is what you see when you look into the mirror: an image of yourself. When God created you, He made you to be a mini version of Himself. If we are to reflect someone well, it would be in our best interest to spend a lot of time with him. You're part of the royal family of God. You're not a monkey, an evolved amoeba, or an accident. You're a daughter of God!

Over the last few years, God has been teaching me that He's not interested in who we think we're supposed to be. He's not interested in who other people think we're supposed to be. When we look in the mirror in the morning and find things to hate, it hurts Him. When we try to be perfect by other people's standards or what we see on television, we sell ourselves short of the love God gives to us freely. Perfectionism comes out of a heart that thinks we know better than God, and it will destroy you. I've been there—it almost destroyed me.

While I was growing up, I had all this knowledge in my head about who I thought Jesus was, and who I thought I was, and what I thought He did, but I was afraid of Him. I didn't pray much, because I was too ashamed— ashamed of not being perfect. I felt like I was walking around with "not good enough" engraved into my forehead

... and nobody told me that Jesus was waiting for me, anyway. He wasn't waiting for me to memorize more Bible verses, or to look prettier, or do better in school. He wanted to love me. One day He made that extra clear when He whispered to me: "You don't belong to religion; you belong to Me. You no longer need to chase perfection; I've already made you perfect."

He wanted me. Just me. And he wants you too. He is waiting for you. He loves you. He doesn't just love you—He so loves you! He identifies with your sufferings, and He celebrates with your victories.

Being assured of His love for you, I challenge you, oh daughter of God, to fight the good fight of faith. Go forth in the knowledge that nothing and no one can compare to how perfectly beautiful you are in the sight of the King.

chapter two

An Identity Crisis

It's so important to have your own relationship with the Lord. That is the number one thing I would say. Be sure that you are getting to a place where God is your best friend. He wants that relationship with you. He wants you to be in love with Him like that. It takes time. It takes discipline to spend time in His Word and spend time listening to stuff that's going to pour life into you and not just thinking about your appearance or things that a lot of music tries to tell you to do. Be careful of that. Be careful of what you're filling your spirit with.[3]
KARI JOBE

THERE WAS A LONG PERIOD IN MY LIFE WHEN I WAS A CHRISTIAN, BUT my foundation was not set in God. There was also a period in my life when I didn't fully understand my identity. I was like the lost and wandering sheep, not knowing where my home was.

I remember the first time I experienced God's presence. I was at a lake in beautiful Muskoka when I heard Him say to me through the waves: "Sarah, I'm not done with you yet. Will you choose Me?

Hold on to Me." I couldn't help but think, *Even the waters speak His name!* I'd never felt so much peace in my life. It was like a shot of joy went right through me. I realized that day I needed to make God my first love and be completely His. I decided to choose Him above everything ... even myself. When God is my first love, my foundation is grounded, my mind is set, and I become unshakable.

In the beginning, our identity was stolen from us. God made Adam and Eve to be the product of a divine creation. He gave them a perfect garden in which to live together and grow in His love. Eve was the first woman born into this world, and the first woman to be made perfect in God's sight. Eve was complete because she knew her identity rested in God alone. She had a good home, perfect peace, no pain, and a loving husband. The only request God made of Eve and Adam was to not eat any fruit from the forbidden Tree of Life; however, one day Eve was in the garden and was tempted to eat from this tree:

> *When the woman* [Eve] *saw that the tree was good for food and pleasing to the eye, and also desirable for gaining wisdom, she took some and ate it. She also gave some to her husband, who was with her, and he ate it. Then the eyes of both of them were opened, and they realized they were naked; so they sewed fig leaves together and made coverings for themselves.* (Genesis 3:6–7)

God gave Adam and Eve the choice of being completely His and to live in a garden full of everything good and perfect. When temptation crept in, Eve took a bite from the apple of the Tree of Life and everything changed. From that moment, generation upon generation would be separated from God. Since that moment in time, we've had an identity crisis.

The Firm Foundation

People are empty and longing for Jesus Christ, yet so many of them ignore God's truth or don't even understand the love and hope that comes from knowing Christ. Who is your identity in? What is your foundation?

Before this world began, God wanted you. He saw a vision of His people. He chose you. He loves you. The first step in embracing our inner beauty is to completely say "yes" to God and lay Him as our firm foundation: "*For no one can lay any foundation other than the one already laid, which is Jesus Christ,*" (1 Corinthians 3:11). To lay that firm foundation, we have to literally die to our earthy bodies:

> *Since we believe that Christ died for all, we also believe that we have all died to our old life. He died for everyone so that those who receive his new life will no longer live for themselves. Instead, they will live for Christ, who died and was raised for them.* (2 Corinthians 5:14–15, NLT)

In January of 2014, I attended a "Time to Be Holy" conference. I had no idea what to expect from this weekend, but I knew I would be growing in God somehow. It was on the last night while we were all in worship that everything changed for me. Danielle Strickland, the motivational speaker for the evening, asked us to die to ourselves and rise up in new life with Christ. *Now wait a minute*, I thought, *I am already a Christian. I asked Jesus into my heart years ago. Why would I need to die to myself?* Somewhere inside of me, the Holy Spirit was pressing me to go up and claim this victory. When it was my turn, I positioned my body on the ground, and Danielle put a black blanket over me. She said these words: "I choose to die to myself and the world and to accept God instead." I repeated the words out loud. Danielle took the blanket off and said, "Rise, child in Christ." I stood up and the peace and grace of God filled my whole being. I died to myself, but I was made alive with Christ.

When I went back home everything was normal. I went back to my normal school, normal church, and normal family. I became so busy with school and church events that I reached the point where I was doing them mostly for myself and not for God. One morning I woke up with a lump in my stomach. *I just can't live this way anymore*, I thought. I'd become so burnt out because I was trying to do everything on my own strength. I felt God asking me: "Sarah, are you going to live for Me or for the world? You cannot do both." In Matthew 16:24–25, Jesus says:

> *If any of you wants to be my follower, you must give up your own way, take up your cross, and follow me. If you try to hang on to your life, you will lose it. But if you give up your life for my sake, you will save it.* (NLT)

I had died to myself at the conference, but once I went back home, I started to live the same kind of life that I had before. I realized that in order to be made alive in Christ, I had to literally die and surrender to God every day. I've learned that when my foundation is in Christ, God will always be there to help me get back up on my feet again when trials come my way or when impossibilities creep in. I may fall, but I'll be falling into the arms of Jesus.

Why is it so important to have our foundation in God? Because everything builds on top of our foundation. Without God as the stronghold, we won't be able to live our life in the way God designed us to, and eventually we'll tumble and fall:

> *So why do you keep calling me "Lord, Lord!" when you don't do what I say? I will show you what it's like when someone comes*

to me, listens to my teaching, and then follows it. It is like a person building a house who digs deep and lays the foundation on solid rock. When the floodwaters rise and break against that house, it stands firm because it is well built. But anyone who hears and doesn't obey is like a person who builds a house right on the ground, without a foundation. When the floods sweep down against that house, it will collapse into a heap of ruins. (Luke 6:46–49, NLT)

Everyone puts their hope and trust in something, whether it's money, school, popularity, boys, or technology. I'm asking you to set your foundation on the solid rock of God. The storms and trials of this life will still come, but with God, you will become unshakeable: "*He alone is my rock and my salvation, my fortress where I will never be shaken,*" (Psalm 62:2, NLT).

Who Is God?

Part of our identity crisis stems from our efforts to make God fit into our own image. When we start making God into our own image, we start believing in a God who is just as messed up as we are. We find our identity by defining and knowing who Christ truly is through Scripture.

God is many things. He is my light in the darkness. He is my peace in the midst of trials and temptation. He is my grace when I don't deserve a second chance. He is my father and the provider of my needs. He is my rest when I am worn. He is the song I sing. He is the strength to my every day. He is my hope and gift of eternal life. You see, He is everything I am not. He is perfect. He is blameless. He is above me and beyond me. He is God. Instead of trying to fit God into my own image, I must work at striving for His image. We must all strive for His likeness. The psalmist writes:

When I consider your heavens, the work of your fingers, the moon and the stars, which you have set in place, what is mankind that you are mindful of them, human beings that you care for them? You have made them a little lower than the angels and crowned them with glory and honor. You made them rulers over the works of your hands; you put everything under their feet: all flocks and herds, and the animals of the wild, the birds in the sky, and the fish in the sea, all that swim the paths of the seas. (Psalm 8:3–8)

God is amazing. Not everyone will know Him. Not everyone will understand Him. God is the answer to everything, but He is also the search, the exploration, and the adventure. Will you find Him today? Will you seek Him out? How amazing it would be to put our full identity and foundation in the God who made the heavens and the earth.

Christ is the visible image of the invisible God. He existed before anything was created and is supreme over all creation, for through Him God created everything … He existed before anything else, and he holds all creation together … He is the beginning, supreme over all … He made peace with everything in heaven and on earth… (Colossians 1:15–18, 20, NLT)

God loves you so much. Some of you have never been told "I love you" by anyone. Maybe you can't fathom that someone—especially God—could love and accept you with all your failures and weaknesses.

I want you to know that God loves you. He doesn't compare us, but He loves us all the same. He created you in your mother's womb. He knew you before your parents even saw you. He forgives when we ask for it and forgets about it before we fall asleep at night. He disciplines us because He is our Father and has the power over tomorrow. He is everything that is good in this life. I dare you to believe that God loves you.

Are you ready to establish your foundation and identity in Christ alone? Maybe you still need to make a commitment to Christ. Closer to the end of this chapter, I'll be going over the steps to salvation and what it truly means to follow Christ and be completely His.

Becoming Completely His

On that day in beautiful Muskoka, God's love broke through to me. I was drifting through life without knowing what it truly meant to give God 100 per cent of myself. I was satisfied with only giving God 90 per cent. I failed to recognize that pure joy would grow deep in my soul when I became completely His. When I said "yes" to God and became completely His, a joy was born down deep in my soul. When I say joy, I don't mean I was "happy" all the time, because happiness is something the world gives me. Happiness is only temporary and circumstantial. Being joy-filled rests in what God gives me, because I chose Him above all else. When this pure joy is born out of God, I still find my joy in God no matter what comes my way.

You don't become more precious on the day you graduate from high school. You don't become more valuable the minute you figure out your career path, and you don't become more meaningful when you get your first boyfriend. Your value comes only from Christ and the truth that God made you. You are already precious, meaningful, and more valuable than you may possibly know to the Creator of everything and the One who holds you in the palms of His hands. You are treasured by Him. Oh girls, I truly hope you realize this amazing kind of living. You are held in the highest form of love, and nothing and no one in this world will ever be able to take that away from you.

No matter where you are or what stage of life you are in, it is never too late to say "yes" to God and become completely His.

I'm asking you today to not just call yourself a Christian, but to step into a relationship with God where you can experience Him as your first love, foundation, and identity. Over 2,000 years ago, God sent His son, Jesus Christ, to this world. Jesus spent the thirty years of his life in total surrender to God. God sent His son to earth to die in our place. You see, without God, we're merely sinners and our identity is lost forever, but with God we have the hope for salvation and eternal life.

I wonder how Jesus endured laying down His life for us. I wonder how He endured all that whipping, all that beating, and all those people yelling, "Crucify Him! Crucify Him!" Then He had to carry that heavy cross to His death. Along the way people mocked Him, spat at Him, and betrayed Him, yet He died for you and me. Three days later, He rose again. Even the grave could not hold Him! Sometimes I can't believe that the Creator of it all laid down His life for me. That's how much He loves you.

In the summer of 2016, I went to Israel and walked the roads Jesus walked 2,000 years ago. The Jesus story became more alive in me as I saw the Sea of Galilee, the hometown of Jesus, the Palm Sunday walk, and the hill where Jesus gave His all so you and I can have salvation and eternal life. His love is real, and when you realize that, no one can ever take it away from you!

If you have a longing to become completely His, take some time to settle this with God. I do want to give you a warning here—you must have your own faith and relationship with God. Too many people are living behind other people's faith, thinking that because their parent or best friend has a good faith, they're okay too. This is a lie. I'm asking you today to step out and decide to say your own "yes" to Jesus.

1. Realize that you're a sinner and in need of a Saviour.

"For everyone has sinned; we all fall short of God's glorious standard," (Romans 3:23, NLT).

2. Believe that eternal life is given to you because of Jesus Christ.

"For the wages of sin is death, but the free gift of God is eternal life through Christ Jesus our Lord," (Romans 6:23, NLT).

3. Recognize that Jesus is God's son and paid the penalty for your sins.

"But God showed His great love for us by sending Christ to die for us while we were still sinners," (Romans 5:8, NLT).

4. Confess and believe. Here you need to ask God to forgive you from your sins.

If you openly declare that Jesus is Lord and believe in your heart that God raised Him from the dead, you will be saved. For it is by believing in your heart that you are made right with God, and it is by openly declaring your faith that you are saved. (Romans 10:9–10)

5. Ask God to save you, and surrender your life to Him.

"For everyone who calls on the name of the Lord will be saved," (Romans 10:13, NLT).

You may also pray this prayer:

Dear God, I realize I am a sinner in need of your grace. I believe that Jesus Christ is your son and was sent to die for my sins. I ask you to forgive me from all my sins and help me to live a better life. Today, I hand over my life to be completely yours.

Remain Completely His

Being completely God's is not a one-time decision, but a life-long process. It's a daily choice and a daily surrender. Remember my story of when I died to myself but went on living my normal life, like nothing had changed? I have to daily surrender my life to God so I can be completely His all over again. Here is a glimpse of what happens when we remain completely His:

LOST IDENTITY	COMPLETELY HIS
Lost and wandering	Found
Rejected by man	Chosen by God
Questioning purpose	Saved by grace
Living in sin	Forgiven
Dead	Alive
Falling into the arms of the world	Unshakable on the firm foundation of God
Darkness	Light

I call it grace. The only reason we are here is because of His marvellous grace. God is not finished with you yet. He will continue to mold you as you grow older and mature. I pray you experience new life and new hope found in Him: "... *O Lord, you are our Father. We are the clay, and you are the potter. We are all formed by your hand*," (Isaiah 64:8, NLT).

As you read this book and live out your daily life, God is molding and forming you: "'*For I know the plans I have for you,' declares the LORD, 'plans to prosper you and not to harm you, plans to give you hope and a future,*'" (Jeremiah 29:11).

This used to be my favourite verse. Knowing that God has a plan for me and a hope for my future motivated me through the hardest times. It gave me strength and helped me to keep wanting to remain completely His. However, this verse is only half of it. Jeremiah 29:13 says: "*You will seek me and find me when you seek me with all your heart.*" Our job is to seek after God with all of our heart and mind. He has a hope and a future planned out for you! This is so exciting! You are now on the incredible adventure I call faith. I pray and hope that you have decided to be completely His today. Allow God to mold and shape you. Isaiah 49:15–16 tells us that God will not forget us and that He has written our names on the palm of His hand.

Adventure Called Faith

WHAT:
An amazing adventure to discover that, through Christ, you are more precious than gold. An amazing adventure to know and believe that God is our beauty mark. This adventure called faith is all about knowing you were created for an extraordinary life.

WHEN:
This adventure begins the moment you say "yes" to God and become completely His.

WHERE:
It all starts with God and is rooted into every aspect of our being.

HOW:
By placing God higher than life itself.

WHAT TO BRING:
- An open heart and mind to escape into the unknown
- Your Bible; it is your road map to where you need to go
- Prayerful and thankful attitude
- Journal—write down what you learn and what your goals are.
- God—make sure you invite Him in and ask Him to be involved in every step.

God, Jesus, and Now the Holy Spirit

I went through a lot of my Christian walk not really understanding the Holy Spirit. I knew about the Trinity and believed that God, Jesus, and the Holy Spirit existed as one, but no one took the time to teach me about the importance of the Holy Spirit. We often talk about God and Jesus, but the Holy Spirit is just as important. When we accept God into our hearts, the Holy Spirit is there as the presence of God on this earth. Jesus tells us in John 14:26: "*But the Advocate, the Holy Spirit, whom the Father will send in my name, will teach you all things and will remind you of everything I have said to you.*"

The Holy Spirit's main job is to bring us closer to God and into His likeness. The Holy Spirit is the One who stirs your heart and mind towards Jesus. He comes into action when you ask God into your heart, take a step of faith, pray to God, or cry out for help. He is ever present and He is everywhere.

My life can sometimes seem so out of control. I want everything to go my way, and I'll try my hardest to make that possible. My life is just one big puzzle that I wish I could figure out right here, right now. But that's not what God does. He only allows us to see and know a certain amount, because He's the only one who knows what tomorrow will bring. He's the author of my story, and the lamp on my path. God is in control. Everything happens in His timing. His ways are always higher and greater than I can ever imagine. Even though I wish I could have everything in my control, I'm so grateful that I don't hold my own future.

> *"My thoughts are nothing like your thoughts," says the Lord. "And my ways are far beyond anything you could imagine. For just as the heavens are higher than the earth, so my ways are higher than your ways and my thoughts higher than your thoughts."* (Isaiah 55:8–9, NLT)

I pray and hope you can rest your future in God's hands. Oh dear one, He has so much more in store of you … beyond anything you could possibly imagine right now. God is holding your puzzle together too, putting all the pieces in place when He sees fit. I know the greatest adventure lies just ahead.

Be Empowered
I have been crucified with Christ and I no longer live, but Christ lives in me. The life I now live in the body, I live by

faith in the Son of God, who loved me and gave himself for me. (Galatians 2:20)

"For the wages of sin is death, but the gift of God is eternal life in Christ Jesus our Lord," (Romans 6:23).

"My grace is all you need. My power works best in your weakness." So now I am glad to boast about my weaknesses, so that the power of Christ can work through me. That's why I take pleasure in my weaknesses and in the insults, hardships, persecutions, and troubles that I suffer for Christ. For when I am weak, then I am strong. (2 Corinthians 12:9–10, NLT)

"Create in me a clean heart, O God, and renew a right spirit within me," (Psalm 51:10, ESV).

"Jesus answered, 'I am the way and the truth and the life,'" (John 14:6).

Thought to Ponder

TO THE GIRL WHO IS LOVED BY THE CREATOR OF THE WORLD (ALL OF YOU!)

BY: REBECCA REIMER

I was fourteen the year *High School Musical* came out and millions of girls fell in love with Zac Efron. I must have watched that DVD twenty or thirty times! As I was watching, I realized that unlike most of the characters in the musical, I didn't have a specific identity. I thought that if I was going to be normal that needed to change, so I decided to be a skater chick. Skateboarding was becoming a popular sport at the time and was something I thought I could do. I went out and bought the clothes and looked the part for when I went back to school. I soon discovered that skateboarding was not only fun, but it got me lots of attention from the boys at my school.

Becoming a skateboarder would have been fine, but it made me realize how quickly I could change myself to fit in. I soon developed an unhealthy way of making friends, particularly boys. If I met a boy I liked, I became what he liked. If he liked cars, I became an expert; if he loved a genre of music, I would download it. I did this for years without even realizing it. I remember graduating from high school and thinking, *What now? I don't even know who I am apart from these people. How am I going to figure out what I want to do with my life?*

I decided to spend a year at Steinbach Bible College to study God's Word and find out who I was. I also made the decision not to date during my time there, because I didn't want to be distracted. It was a great year. I made girlfriends who will be with me for my whole life. I discovered that I loved music and ministry and so much more, because I wasn't trying to impress anyone or fit in.

But what I learned about my identity in God changed my life. When I realized how much He loves me and wants what's best for me, I didn't need the approval of my peers. I realized that it didn't matter what I wore or listened to, or where I lived—God's love for me is never going to change! I was free to be exactly who He created me to be. Knowing who I am in God affects the way I live. When I know how much I'm loved by the Creator of the world, I live life loving everyone around me. I don't discriminate. I live confidently and don't feel like I need to change myself to get approval from others. People change, but God never does!

When I see the grace that God has given to me, I can be gracious to others when they hurt me. Who I am no longer depends on the people I hang out with or what I wear, because I know who I am in God. I am loved and accepted by the King of the Universe! I'm praying that as you read this book you will comprehend how much God loves you, and that this knowledge will spill into everything you are!

P.S. While I was busy searching after God, He was preparing a wonderful husband for me. Trevor and I both decided to take that year to study God's Word. My commitment to being single during that year of school made it possible for me to become who Trevor was looking for in a wife. We're now married and have two beautiful children who make us laugh every day! So girls, continue seeking after God with all your heart. He has more in store for you than you can imagine. While He crafts and designs your future, look to Him for your identity in everything.

chapter three

Making Him
the Centre of It All

For beautiful eyes, look for the good in others;
for beautiful lips, speak only words of kindness;
and for poise, walk with the knowledge
that you are never alone.[4]
AUDREY HEPBURN

ONE OF THE WAYS I DRAW CLOSE TO GOD IS THROUGH MUSIC. EVERY time a worship song comes on, I focus on the words and pray them into my own life. This past week, I played the piano chords to the song "Heart of Worship" by Matthew Redman. As I played, I started to sing the lyrics, which begin with, "When the music fades, all is stripped away …" I started to think to myself, *When the music fades and all is stripped away, can I still worship God without the song? Can I still offer all that I am to God, even when I'm not singing in church?* You see, God searches deep within—so deep that He calls us to not just worship when we're singing a praise song on Sunday, but to worship Him in every aspect of our lives. I want to give God more than a song. How about you?

Worship Is a Lifestyle

I have learned along this adventure that the best way to live is to set God higher than life itself. This means that worship has to be a lifestyle. Isn't it amazing how God doesn't just want us on Sunday, but that He wants us when we're at work, at school, taking a test, eating dinner with our family, or when we're alone in our room? Worship is how you and I live out our lives, moment by moment, and minute by minute.

When we make worship our lifestyle, we are saying to God: *I want to place you, O Lord, higher than life itself. Your ways are better; your ways are higher. Teach me your ways that I may bring you glory and honour the rest of my days.* Be aware, though, that we can worship anything, even if it has nothing to do with God. If we aren't focused on worshipping and glorifying Christ alone, we start to worship idols, such as materialistic objects and other things this world offers us. We must be authentic with our worship and seek to glorify God alone.

One of my favourite ways to worship is to be in fellowship with my friends. One day nine of us decided to hike to the most southern part of Canada: Point Pelee. We hiked for about five kilometres. During our time together, we laughed, shared stories, and grew in the Lord. Once we were finished the hike, we decided it was too early to end the day, so we all went back to my house for a good meal and more fellowship. We talked about the true meaning of worship and what worshipping God is all about. Throughout the full conversation, we realized our whole day was spent in worship. As we hiked, as we shared our stories, and as we ate our dinner together, we were worshipping God. We realized that we must continue worshipping God every day.

Prayer and God's Word

If we want to embrace our inner beauty and become all God created us to be, we need to talk to God on a regular basis. We cannot simply say to ourselves, "I'm going to embrace my inner beauty and leave God out of the whole process." No, we must pray to God and depend on Him every step of the way. A friend once told me, "We cannot call ourselves a Christian if we do not pray and read our Bible."

We need to pray without ceasing. This means I pray throughout my day, every day. I pray in the car when I see a family quarrelling in their driveway. I pray when I see a lonely man on the bench. I pray when I'm about to give a speech. I pray before I travel on a plane or a train. I try to include God in every aspect of my life.

When I was younger, I had trouble remembering to pray, or even wanting to pray, so instead of praying out loud, I started to journal my prayers. I'd write letters to God about thanksgiving and about my needs and doubts. I still journal my prayers to this day, and it's the best way I pray to God. Find out how you can pray the best and stick with it. God wants to hear from you. Will you invite God into all aspects of your life?

Meditation involves opening our minds to God's Word and what He might want us to learn from it. The key to meditation is never to rush it. Eliminate and remove all distractions and take time to get your mind back in focus as soon as it starts wandering. Another great way to meditate is to keep a journal of everything you learn and what God says to you during your quiet time. When I want to meditate, I spend about five to ten minutes on five verses at a time. I don't read any more than five, but I read those five verses over and over again until they are woven into my mind. They might not be memorized yet, but I'm on my way.

Something amazing happens when we meditate and memorize God's Word. Psalm 139:7 asks: "*Where can I go from your Spirit? Where can I flee from your presence?*" Memorizing scripture can be hard, but it has lasting rewards. I memorized a lot of scripture back in grade school. Some of it has faded, but some of it comes back into my mind the minute I need it. Memorization unlocks the freedom to carry the

Bible around in your mind wherever you go. It's there when you're helping a friend, being a witness to a stranger, or even when you're going through a hard time. Memorization also identifies who Christ truly is and helps you live it out in a better way.

Here are some tips for memorizing the Bible:

1. Start slow. Don't try to memorize a whole chapter at one time. Pick your favourite verses and work on it.
2. Repetition. Say your verses over and over again, and post them around your house so you see them daily.
3. Start with memorizing your favourite worship song that incorporates scripture. This one is fun!

Lysa TerKerust is the director of Proverbs 31 Ministries. She is an author and a national speaker. She has given us five simple questions to help us filter the Bible as we read it, so that we can properly understand what God is telling us.

1. Who is the passage speaking to?
2. What is it saying to me?
3. What direction is this passage giving?
4. How might I need to change my way of thinking or acting as a result of this verse?
5. What are some other verses that relate to this topic, both in the Old Testament and in the New Testament?[5]

Practice His Presence

In a world that's always so busy and noisy, it's hard to take our attention off our chaotic lives and draw close to God. We try to fit God into our already-busy schedules, leaving Him with only a few minutes out of our day. We can't worship God completely if we don't take the time to be with Him. Are you going to take the time to draw close to God? Are you paying attention?

I want to share with you some exercises to help you practice His presence. The goal is not to do all of them at once, but to take one and practice it for a whole week. During the second week, add one more on top of the one you've already chosen. Continue and repeat until practicing His presence becomes a natural part of your daily life.

1. Start with scripture. God's presence becomes more real for me when I read His Word. In Jeremiah 29:13, God tells us: "*You will seek me and find me, when you seek me with all your heart*," (ESV).

   Lead me in your truth and teach me, for you are the God of my salvation; for you I wait all the day long. Remember your mercy, O LORD, and your steadfast love, for they have been from of old ... He leads the humble in what is right, and teaches the humble his way. (Psalm 25:5–6, 9, ESV)

   "So faith comes from hearing, and hearing through the word of Christ," (Romans 10:17, ESV).

   You will find Him when you seek for Him with all of your heart through God's Word.

2. Put your phone down. We carry our phones with us everywhere. We spend every spare second scrolling through Facebook, Instagram, and other social media apps. Instead of being on your phone, sit or stand and talk to God in those moments. You can pray things like:
   "God be with me today."
   "What are you trying to show me today?"
   "How can I best serve you today?"
   These types of prayers get your mind to focus on what truly matters. Make it a habit to pray instead of scrolling through your phone.

3. Make the time. You must make time for God. It's called time management and self-discipline. I put a reminder on my day planner to start the day with God and end the day with God. Some days I still forget, but the extra reminder helps me to know He is the priority of every day.

4. Whenever you have a big test, speech, or task ahead, talk to God about it before you start. Invite Him in and talk to Him during the task. God loves it when we seek Him first.

5. Sing songs of praise throughout the day. You can sing it to yourself or put on the radio. This one is my favourite, because God speaks to me through the words, and the beat gets me very excited and motivated.

6. Write out prayers of praise and thanksgiving and stick them around your house, room, locker, or car where you can see them every day. Repeat them daily.

7. Journal your thoughts. Write love letters of thanksgiving to God. Pour out your heart to Him on paper.

8. Make up your own ways to practice God's presence. Be creative. If you have any tips for practicing His presence, please take the time to add those to this list and even write to me. We can learn from each other.

Surrender, Solitude, and Silence

It's hard to get peace and quiet around here! My house always seems to be loud. With six people living here, a music studio, two dogs, and a lot of fellowship nights, it can be hard to find solitude and silence with God. However, solitude, silence, and surrender are the key to survival.

Surrender is the first step to solitude and silence. I surrender by literally saying, "God, I cannot do this on my own. I need you in every aspect of my life." I have to start my day with God before I turn on my phone, have a shower, or start work. I usually pray and then read scripture. This helps focus my heart and reminds me to trust in God no matter what happens in that day. Will you surrender your day to God?

Here are my steps to solitude and silence:

1. Take a day trip with God. I shut off my phone, computer, and any other technology and simply have a date with Him. My favourite kind of day is going for a long drive, windows down as I cry my heart out to God. I tell Him everything that's on my mind. It always feels so good, because I know He's listening and I have no distractions. My drive usually takes me to a lake where I take off my shoes and wade in the water. I ask God to forgive my sins as I list them for Him. I then listen. I listen to the sound of His voice through the wind and waves. I wade in the water until I'm refreshed by knowing I spent quality time with my God.

2. Start the time of silence and solitude by saying, "Here I am, Lord. I'm listening. Speak to me, for I am here." If it helps, put your timer on for ten minutes. Even if you don't "hear" His voice, sit there in silence. Repeat this until it works for you.

3. Bow. There's something about coming into a quiet room and kneeling before God. I take off my shoes and simply bow. I take time to talk and pray to God as well as bow in silence waiting for Him to speak.

4. Again, read scripture. Make scripture a part of everything!

5. Make up your own. Be creative. Maybe instead of going to a lake you want to fish, hike, or skate. Whatever it is, make solitude and silence a priority in your life.

Be Committed to Your Church

In order to continue drawing closer to God, stay committed to your local church. Whether it's Baptist, Reformed, Pentecostal, nondenominational, Anglican, Catholic, or The Salvation Army, be there on Sunday. Just like people go to school to study, we all need church to teach us the truths of drawing closer to God. God doesn't want us just to attend church—He wants us actively involved in our church. Paul instructs us:

> *For just as each of us has one body with many members, and these members do not all have the same function, so in Christ we, though many, form one body, and each member belongs to all the others. We have different gifts, according to the grace given to each of us. If your gift is prophesying, then prophesy in accordance with your faith; if it is serving, then serve; if it is teaching, then teach; if it is to encourage, then give encouragement; if it is giving, then give generously; if it is to lead, do it diligently; if it is to show mercy, do it cheerfully … cling to what is good. Be devoted to one another in love; honor one another above yourselves.* (Romans 12:4–10)

You and I are called to be a part of the body of a church. We have the chance to grow together in a church family. Isn't that beautiful? I encourage you to start thinking today about how you can serve God in your church. The possibilities are endless:

1. Start an outreach ministry for the homeless.
2. Become a Sunday school leader.
3. Volunteer where you are needed (youth programs, children's programs, or elderly programs).
4. Start a new program for your church.
5. Have a "girls' night" for the younger girls at your church to teach them about God and His love for them.
6. Mentor someone.
7. Sing in the worship band.

8. Start a fundraiser to go on a missions trip.

9. Make up your own.

As you start to grow with your church family, you'll understand why it's so important. Whatever it is, I pray and hope you experience the joy of being involved and committed to church.

Sin and Temptation

Sin and temptation are a part of the Christian walk, just as much as joy and laughter are. Temptation means being drawn to do something unwise or wrong. Sin occurs when we act out that temptation and refuse to accept God's way over our own way. It flows from decisions, thoughts, and actions. Sin rejects God's truth and instead drives us to steal, curse, lie, and dishonour God. It creeps in when we start to believe Satan's lies and deception. In *A Purpose Driven Life*, Rick Warren outlines a few steps to enduring sin and temptation.

1. Refuse to be intimidated. Refuse to be fearful. The lie of Satan says you will never be able to outgrow sin, so don't even try.

2. Recognize that temptation is not the sin—it's what we do with the temptation that can cause the sin.

3. Do not justify the sin. For example, if we tell a lie and no one catches us the first time, we lie again and again until we don't think there's anything wrong with it anymore. This is because we've justified the sin.

4. Stay alert. Be prepared for the temptation so that you'll reject the sin.

5. View every temptation as an opportunity to do good. Remember, God will always provide a way out of the temptation.

6. Forgive. Do not live in sin; forgive yourself and ask God for forgiveness.[6]

Paul says it all in 1 Corinthians 10:13:

No temptation has overtaken you except what is common to mankind. And God is faithful; he will not let you be tempted beyond what you can bear. But when you are tempted, he will also provide a way out so that you can endure it.

"God blesses those who patiently endure testing and temptation. Afterward they will receive the crown of life that God has promised to those who love Him," (James 1:12, NLT).

I pray and hope you look to Jesus when you're in the midst of temptation. He will go before you.

Who It Really Frees Is You

"Be kind and compassionate to one another, forgiving each other, just as in Christ God forgave you," (Ephesians 4:23).

God is the Father of forgiveness, as He laid down His life for our sins. Forgiveness needs to be a part of our life if we want to serve God. Forgiveness can be hard, especially when our world tells us it's okay to hold grudges and to pay back those who hurt us. I believe we should live differently: *"... leave it to the wrath of God, for it is written, 'Vengeance is mine, I will repay, says the Lord,'"* (Romans 12:19, ESV). Jesus commands us to, *"Do good to those who hate you, bless those who curse you, pray for those who abuse you,"* (Luke 6:27–28, ESV).

We are all equal; we have all sinned and fallen short of God's glory. We're no better than the person who needs our forgiveness. How do we forgive people who hurt us so deeply? How do we pray for those who hurt us over and over again? We forgive by praying and handing the situation over to God, taking the time to cool down, taking time to think about the whole picture, and always remembering that God forgave us. When we forgive someone, we don't have to forget what that person did, but we do need to show the same love God showed us: "*Don't think you are better than you really are. Be honest in your evaluation of yourselves, measuring yourselves by the faith God has given us*," (Romans 12:3, NLT); "*Do not repay evil for evil. Don't retaliate with insults when people insult you. Instead, pay them back with a blessing*," (1 Peter 3:9, NLT).

Sometimes it's harder to forgive because we think the person doesn't deserve our forgiveness. When you live this way, you're living in bondage. If you hold a grudge, you'll miss out on the joyful life God meant for you to have. When you decide to forgive, the person who you truly free is yourself. "*So if the Son sets you free, you will be free indeed*," (John 8:36, ESV). Did you catch that? Free indeed—meaning you no longer live in that kind of bondage.

The next time you're struggling to forgive someone, remember what God did for us on the cross. Remember that God is the Father of forgiveness, and we must live that truth out in our own lives. The key to forgiveness is understanding that we cannot ask God to forgive us if we aren't willing to forgive others.

Will you pray for those who hurt you? Will you love the person, even in light of the wrong they have done? I encourage you to be kind and forgive each other, just as God forgave you.

You've Got to Have Faith

I've talked about this amazing adventure called "faith." Now it's time to carefully identify what this really means. Faith … ah, this is my favourite word! Once we claim Jesus Christ as our Lord and King of our hearts, we have to grow. How do we grow? By faith. For faith believes in what is yet to come. Faith is the hope for what is not yet seen. Stated another way, God-driven women believe and know their dreams will come true before they actually do. God says in His Word that we can tell Him our plans, but He will always determine our steps. Will you let Him?

Faith and actions work together. This is seen throughout the book of Hebrews. I encourage you to pick up your Bibles, read through the book of Hebrews, and make your own notes. How does faith work? Why do faith and actions work together? How can you put your faith into action today? For now, I will share my notes about faith with you.

Our actions make our faith complete. Although we are saved by believing in God alone, once we make that decision, our lives must reflect that promise. Just like our bodies would be dead if we didn't breathe, our faith is dead unless we put it into action and make our lives reflect Christ. How can we show God we believe in Him? How can we share the good news with others? By living out faith in everything we do.

Do Not Drift Away

Hebrews 2:1–3 contains a warning about drifting away:

So we must listen very carefully to the truth we have heard, or we may drift away from it. For the message of God delivered through angels has always stood firm, and every violation of the law and every act of disobedience was punished. So what makes us think we can escape if we ignore this great salvation that was first announced by the Lord Jesus himself and then delivered to us by those who heard him speak? (NLT)

James says it more clearly:

What is causing the quarrels and fights among you? Don't they come from the evil desires at war within you? You want what you don't have, so you scheme and kill to get it. You are jealous of what others have, but you can't get it, so you fight and wage war to take it away from them ... so humble yourselves before God. Resist the devil [worldly temptations]*, and he will flee from you. Come close to God, and God will come close to you. Wash your hands... purify your hearts.* (James 4:1–2, 7, NLT)

I want to share with you my eight steps to help keep me from drifting away:

1. Wake up and greet God every morning with a prayer, inviting Him into your day.
2. Read scriptures as if they are love letters just for you.
3. Make time every day to have devotions and silent time with God.
4. Pray without ceasing.
5. See each person you meet as an opportunity to share God's love.
6. Hug and kiss friends and members of your family regularly.
7. Smile and stay positive.
8. Before turning the light out, pray with God again, thanking Him for the day.

Be that woman who hopes for God to guide her every day. Psalms 25:4–5 says:

Show me your ways, Lord, teach me your paths. Guide me in your truth and teach me, for you are God my Savior, and my hope is in you all day long.

An Active Follower of Christ

1. She knows that with God, it is a relationship not a religion.
2. She puts her faith into action.
3. She has a good support system of Christian friends and leaders.
4. She prays.
5. She never stops growing.
6. She lives according to God's Word.
7. She knows she belongs to God and not the world.
8. She encourages and supports others in their walk with God.

You Need a Best Friend

For some reason, God decided to not give me any biological sisters. I struggled with this growing up, as I always wanted a sister I could share my clothes with, tell my secrets to, and just do life with. Instead, I was given two crazy twin brothers. I love them dearly, but I still needed a girl in my life I could call my sister. With God, everyone is a family. God has blessed me with amazing friendships and sisters in Christ. I have a solid group of strong women I can go to with my secrets and mistakes, take adventures with, and just have a good ol' laugh with. I want you to realize how important it is to have a best friend in your life.

A true friend is someone you can trust with everything, someone who will be honest with you, someone who will not judge you despite your past mistakes or current struggles, and someone who will encourage you in your walk with Christ. Proverbs 27:9 says, "*The heartfelt counsel of a friend is a sweet as perfume and incense*," (NLT).

We need godly friends in our life. Find someone who chases after God with you and loves Him as much as you do. Also, you must be a best friend to someone. Friendships are two-sided—it takes two people to make a friendship last. A lot of my sisters in Christ don't live in the same city as me. It can be hard to keep our friendship going in this fast-paced world, but true friends know how to make it work through commitment and loyalty.

I encourage you to make sure you have at least two or three mentors in your life to whom you can go for wisdom, advice, and answers to all those tough questions. A mentor can be a youth leader, teacher, pastor, aunt, or someone you look up to. Identify who your friends and mentors are. Claim them as your best friends. Claim them as people you can approach to help you draw closer to God. Just remember that God is the only one who can fill your cup; He is the only one who can fully satisfy your every need. Friends and mentors are simply the overflow of what God already gives us, but they will help us in many ways along this journey.

Be Empowered

"Devote yourselves to prayer with an alert mind and a thankful heart," (Colossians 4:2, NLT).

"The Lord is close to all who call on him, yes, to all who call on him in truth," (Psalm 145:18, NLT).

I am the true vine, and my Father is the gardener. He cuts off every branch in me that bears no fruit, while every branch that does bear fruit he prunes so that it will be even more fruitful. You are already clean because of the word I have spoken to you. Remain in me, as I also remain in you. No branch can bear fruit by itself; it must remain in the vine. Neither can you bear fruit unless you remain in me. (John 15:1–4)

"May the God of hope fill you with all joy and peace as you trust in him …, " (Romans 15:13).

Thought to Ponder
TO THE GIRL WHO IS NEEDING SOME HOPE
BY: CASSIE BARRETT

Hi, my name is Cassie Barrett. I'm nineteen, and I'm studying radiation therapy at McMaster University. This is my story. I was very blessed to grow up in a supportive Christian family, although I realized that I was in the minority and that none of my friends were Christians. For that reason, I always felt different from everyone else. As you can imagine, as a kid it's hard to be different and believe different things. I was almost ashamed to be a Christian.

One Saturday night when I was very young, the neighbourhood kids and I were playing manhunt outside. My sister and I were called in early to go to sleep so that we could wake up early the next morning to go to church. I was quite angry with my mom, and again felt different and excluded from the rest of the kids. I remember asking my mom why we went to church, and she replied with, "Our family loves God, and we want to learn more about Him." I told her that I hated God. After a long pause, she said, "Cassie, I hope you change your mind one day." By my mom's response I could tell that she really did love God, and she really was taking this "God thing" seriously.

A few years later, I went to my church's camp for the first time. There I met about 100 other kids on the same spiritual journey as me, asking the same questions. I met people who lived out their faith and loved being Christians. With the help of these people, and by watching the way they lived their lives, I stopped being ashamed of being a Christian. I can now fearlessly say that I love living out my faith in a world where I'm naturally different from so many people.

Although I now realize that I wasn't alone on my spiritual journey, I also understand what it's like to feel completely alone. But through my experiences, I've learned that God will never leave me alone.

A few years ago, my mom was diagnosed with cancer in her lungs. This was a shock to our family and friends, but throughout this terrible situation, many people prayed for her. I'd never heard of so many people praying for one person. I had complete hope that God could and would heal my mom. Last summer, my mom passed away. I was shocked and so angry with God. I felt alone and betrayed.

At the time of her passing, I was working as a cabin leader at the same summer camp I went to as a kid—the Salvation Army's Camp Newport. A few weeks after my mom passed away, I was leading a devotion for my ten to eleven-year-old campers. It was the story of Job, a man who had everything taken from him, but praised God throughout his sufferings. As I was sharing with the girls that God never left Job, I realized that I wasn't truly believing it myself. After my devotion, one of my campers added to the devotion. She shared that her church had held many prayer meetings for a lady who was sick, but the lady passed away. She then explained that she knew God hadn't forgotten about or ignored their prayers, but had answered them in different ways. The people involved in this situation were blessed, even though the lady passed away. She then added that the lady's name was Heather Barrett. At that moment, I knew God was speaking to me, because that lady was my mom. This camper had never met my mom, and she didn't know me, but she'd been praying for my mom. I knew that God used this moment to help me realize that He'd never left me alone in this situation.

No matter what situation you're in, or where you're at in your life, or what hurt you may be feeling, God will never leave you: "*I am with you always, even to the end of the age*," (Matthew 28:20, NLT).

chapter four

A Holy Temple

I feel very strongly that curves are natural, womanly and real. I shall continue to hope that women are able to believe in themselves for who they are inside, and not feel under such incredible pressure to be unnaturally thin.[7]

KATE WINSLET

GOOD MORNING, WORLD! IT'S TIME TO GET UP AND START THE DAY. I WALK into my bathroom and look in the mirror. *Oh, Sarah, when did you start looking so ugly? You have so much acne. Will it ever go away? Oh, and that nose! It's so huge! Why didn't God give me a smaller nose? Are my hips getting bigger? I guess it's time to step on the scale and see how much weight I've gained …*

Let me let you in on a little secret—no girl wakes up feeling beautiful every single day. Oh, how I wish I could look into the mirror and not point out one thing about myself that I dislike and wish I could change. Guess what? There is a way:

> *Now we see things imperfectly, like puzzling reflections in a mirror, but then we will see everything with perfect clarity. All*

that I know now is partial and incomplete, but then I will know everything completely, just as God now knows me completely. (1 Corinthians 13:12, NLT)

I used to look at my body image and self-worth through a worldly mirror. I became obsessed with food and being thin, to the point where I let it control me. I put restrictions on what I could and could not eat, just so I could stay at the "perfect" weight to "feel" pretty. I used to believe that true beauty only happened when I was a certain weight and had no acne. I'd look at myself in a mirror and only see a broken, ugly, and worthless girl. Since then, I've made peace with my reflection and who God made me to be. God has brought me to perfect clarity, because He is my mirror. It was only through the grace of God I was made whole and complete. I have thrown away my mask and put on my soul. You can too. I hope that today you can move from seeing yourself through a worldly mirror to seeing yourself through God's eyes.

Do you not know that your bodies are temples of the Holy Spirit, who is in you, whom you have received from God? You are not your own; you were bought at a price. Therefore honor God with your bodies. (1 Corinthians 6:19–20)

When we are completely His, our bodies become holy temples of the Holy Spirit, and we need to keep them in good condition so God can work through us the way He desires to.

Loving the Woman in the Mirror

There are two lies that this world tells us. One, it's okay to be completely self-absorbed and vain, and two, to be truly happy, we must pretend to be someone we are not. When we live like this, we live as prisoners inside ourselves. The longer we live like this, the harder it is to escape. I want God to break you free from those chains. I want you to live out that God-fearing life and beauty you possess. I want to caution you first—although truly loving yourself and what God created you to be is important, we must always remember that God still comes first. We must still strive to love Him above ourselves. I simply want you to love the girl you see in the mirror, because you are a child of God.

Body-image, self-esteem, and self-worth come from our evaluations of ourselves and what this world dictates to us. We all have our own definitions of beauty. This world is trying to brainwash us when it comes to the ideal body image. They tell us what we should weigh, how our skin and hair should look, and what type of body to have. The problem is that society's and the world's expectations of body image are always changing. One day everyone wants to be like Beyoncé, and the next day everyone wants to be like Taylor Swift. Where does it end?

It's time to love the woman in the mirror. How can we love God if we don't love ourselves? Does a woman who knows she is deeply loved by God walk around feeling depressed and complaining about her looks? No, not if the love of God has been planted deep in her soul. To truly love God and believe He loves you is to love yourself— all of it. And hold nothing back, girl!

We all have insecurities, so let's stop denying them and start identifying them. What are you insecure about when it comes to your body? Is it your rocking hips? Maybe your acne scars? Or maybe you just compare yourself with others and are envious of their looks? Whatever it is, stop! Remember, there is no one on earth that is like you, and that is pretty amazing. God made no mistakes when He made you. He designed your height, weight, hair colour, and skin tone with a purpose in mind. He designed every part of you for His

49

purpose. Here's what happens when we view ourselves by worldly standards:

1. We never accept ourselves the way God made us.
2. We become our worst critic.
3. We compare ourselves to others.
4. We feel threatened by girls who seem "prettier" than us.
5. We make unnecessary changes to our bodies just to "fit in."
6. We judge others, even if we don't say anything out loud.
7. We are lost.
8. We hide behind a mask.
9. We sometimes look to boys to fill the void and emptiness.
10. We have unrealistic expectations.
11. We start believing the lies of social media and their idea of "the true body image."

I remember going through puberty and walking down the halls of my high school wishing I was someone I was not. I still have to ask myself if I'm hiding behind a mask, or if I'm embracing all God gave me. How about you? How do you view your body and self-image?

Here is how God sees you:

New Creation	2 Corinthians 5:17
Royalty	1 Peter 2:9
Transformed	Romans 12:2
Citizen of Heaven	Philippians 3:20
Light	1 Thessalonians 5:5
Ambassador	2 Corinthians 5:20
Fearfully and Wonderfully Made	Psalms 139
Free in Christ	Romans 6:18
God's Fragrance	2 Corinthians 2:15
Forgiven	John 3:16
Chosen	Romans 8:28

Loved	1 John 4:16
Bold and Brave	Ephesians 3:12
Fulfilled and Complete	Colossians 2:10
His Workmanship	Ephesians 2:10
Holy	Deuteronomy 7:10
Strengthened	Isaiah 41:10
Healed	Isaiah 53:5
Made Complete	Jeremiah 29:11
Redeemed	Colossians 1:12–14

I don't know about you, but when I read these words, I realize that nothing is more amazing than how God makes us beautiful. Want to know another secret? God is the One who makes me beautiful. When I start to judge myself, or when I start to look to others to make me feel beautiful, I ask God to bring me back to the knowledge that in Him, and Him alone, I am forgiven, I am chosen, I am holy, I am strengthened, I am healed, and I am fearfully and wonderfully made. When I remember His truth above my own, I am free from the world's condemnation and what they try to call beautiful. Instead, I walk with the boldness of Christ, knowing I am strong and joy-filled.

God wants you to be you. He wants you to love the skin you're in and every curve of your body. Go stand in front of the mirror and say out loud, "I am a masterpiece. I am radiant. I am chosen. And I am beautiful." In God's eyes, every single body is beautiful, because He made us! The next time you look at a magazine cover and wish you had the body on the front, shake that thinking off and look down at who God made you to be. Adapt Psalm 129:14 to say, "I am beautiful, because God created me," and Jeremiah 17:7–8 to say, "Blessed is the girl who trusts in Me, the woman who sticks with God. She is like a tree replanted in Eden, putting down roots near the river. Never a worry, bearing fresh fruit every season."

In 1 Samuel 16:7b God says, "*People look at the outward appearance, but the LORD looks at the heart.*" Stop stepping on the scale and step instead into God's abundant grace. I hope and pray that God is bringing you to perfect clarity so you can love the woman in *His* mirror. Isn't it beautiful how God looks past our outward appearance and our mistakes and looks deep into our hearts? I'm so thankful I have a God who makes us beautiful. There's no one else on earth who is like you. I think that's pretty amazing.

Stop Comparing Yourself to Others

As women, it's only natural to compare ourselves with each other. *That girl has the hair I want. She looks so good in those jeans. Why can't I look that good? I wish I had clear skin like her.* We've all thought these things before, but that's not how we're supposed to live.

I know one thing for sure—God will never help you become someone you're not. I also know that comparison is the thief of joy. I want to stop comparing myself to others and start celebrating what God has given me! Don't you? Here are some questions I ask myself to remind me that I don't need to compare myself to others:

Do I care for others, or do I care what others think of me?

Am I living for Christ, or am I living for people's approval?

Am I living for the kingdom of me, or the Kingdom of God?

These questions help me every day to turn my thinking from jealousy, envy, and bitterness to reflecting God's radiant grace. When I change my thinking, I don't feel the need to compare myself to others. I'm able to hold my head up high and accept the person I was created to be. This also helps me to admire someone else's beauty without judging my own. I've said it once before, but I need to say it again: instead of focusing so much on what others think of us, let's soak in how much God truly treasures us.

What's in Your Closet?

How we dress tells a lot about our character and love for Jesus. I'm not saying you should never dye your hair, paint your nails, or wear your favourite outfit. Trust me, I love looking good, but that's not where I find my self-worth. I always have to keep in mind that the way I dress informs unbelievers and believers about my character. I want to share with you God's description of a virtuous and worthy woman. 1 Peter 3:3–4 covers this in detail:

> *Do not let your adorning be external—the braiding of hair and putting on of gold jewelry, or the clothing you wear—but let your adorning be the hidden person of the heart with the imperishable beautiful gentle and quiet spirit, which in God's sight is very precious.* (ESV)

This passage states that there's nothing wrong with braiding our hair or wearing nice clothes, but we must seek God first and allow Him to work on us from the inside out. God is showing us that our outer beauty can fade away, but with Him, our inner beauty can last forever. Modesty is important. It's how we carry ourselves, how we respect others, and how we worship God.

1. Modesty doesn't entail being anti-style or anti-fashion. I don't want you to go through your closet and throw out everything and start wearing rags. Enjoy the latest fashions. Enjoy going to the mall with your friends. Just remember to be well-kept, put together, and modest.
2. Modesty shows who or what you are worshipping. Draw attention to God, not yourself.
3. Modesty is about attitude, not just clothing. Modesty is about how we act, think, and interact with others.

4. Modesty reveals how you view yourself. Do you love your body? Do you love your skin? Honour your body.
5. Modesty is about creativity. Who says you have to stick with the latest fashion trends? One of the things I love to do with my girlfriends is to go thrift shopping. Sometimes we find the best deals and make up our own fashions! Be creative and make up your own fashion statement.

The most important thing about modesty is this: Your body wasn't made to be plastered on the billboards and magazine covers wearing nothing but your bra or underwear like Hollywood depicts us. Your body was not made to be seen by everyone at the beach. And your body wasn't made to show off to every guy that passes by. Your body is beautiful, holy, and lovely, but most importantly it is sacred. You owe it to yourself to cover up and save your sacred body. I will talk more about this in chapter five and chapter ten.

It's a tragedy that so many of us obsess over what we wear. The most common compliment we give each other is, "Oh, I just love your shoes! Oh, where did you get that shirt? I absolutely love those ripped jeans." But are you being radical for God by the way you dress? I've even caught myself caring more about how my clothes look than about representing God. My hope and plea is that you take a reality check of your closet and wardrobe. Instead of hitting the mall to buy the latest $300 pair of jeans, take a break from the obsession of clothing and just breathe. Just shut it all off and breathe, take a walk with God, and remember that your worth does not come from the external look of clothes and jewelry, but from who you are in Christ.

I want to share with you a quote from Lysa Terkeurst that I hold dear to my heart:

The mark of a truly godly woman is one who reveals the power of God not so much in her doing as in her being. She has opened God's treasure chest of joy and so filled her heart with gratitude and love that just being around her inspires you. She goes about the simplest of tasks, her everyday duties and even the rough patches of life with such grace that you find yourself wanting to imitate her. She is full of adventure yet not worn out from the journey.[8]

This is such a beautiful example of the kind of godly woman I want to be. I want to strive to be clothed in a way that I can go about the rough patches of life with grace and love, don't you? As for me, I want to be a virtuous woman who loves God by what I wear from the inside out.

So what is in your closet? I encourage you to be wise in your decisions when you go shopping and when you leave the house. What we wear doesn't make us a Christian, but it can be a witness to both believers and unbelievers. I hope you'll look in your closet and see how you can clothe yourself in a way to honour and please God. Have some fun too. Enjoy doing your hair and have fun wearing those heels, but also know what you wear on the inside will be reflected on the outside.

The Issue of Technology

Our world is fixated on self-image. Our culture tells us to have a "selfie" worldview. We see this through Facebook, Instagram, and Snapchat. Can't you see that this world is slowly telling us to take our eyes off God's world and turn it into a "selfie" world? One of the reasons we don't see ourselves with perfect clarity is that we're all so addicted to social media and computer-generated relationships that distract our lives.

Television, video games, and social media are some of the greatest life-wasters of all time. Unfortunately, technology is available at the touch of our fingertips. I love a good movie from time to time, and I even enjoy watching *The Bachelor* with my girlfriends, but we must remember the song that says, "Oh be careful little eyes what you see. Cause the father up above is looking down with love, oh be careful little eyes what you see." The very essence of that song is what I am trying to tell you. What we see and hear on TV shows, movies, music, and video games leaves a lasting impression on our minds. I'm not asking you to live under a rock, but I am giving you a warning that if you and I aren't careful, technology can damage our growth with God in many ways.

You may think that watching a TV show with a lot of swearing or sexual content won't affect your life, but that's a lie. Those images and words affect your thoughts, which in turn affect your words, which then affect your actions, which make up your character. When we see a sexual image, it stays in our brains and repeats in our minds forever. Forever. Even if you watch an episode only once, it can stay active in your brain, which is very unhealthy.

Our society has become immune to what it hears. We have normalized words that are so foul and unholy that they're not even in the dictionary. Your words tell the story of your relationship with Christ. We'll talk later about how we need to speak life, but I want to talk a little about foul language in technology. When I watch a movie that has a lot of swearing and crude language, even if I don't repeat them out loud, the words repeat themselves in my head. And having them in our minds is just as bad as saying them out loud. I want to live in such a way that they don't enter my mind and thinking.

You may be wondering how we can escape these influences when technology, sexual content, and foul language are everywhere. We escape it by setting boundaries and learning the word "no." I encourage you to stand up for what you believe in. I hope you know your values and will stick to them. If you're out with friends and they put on a movie that's dangerous to your system, walk out of the room. If you're with a group of friends who are looking at content they shouldn't, stand up and leave. You may think this will ruin friendships, but your true friends will respect you. You may even influence them to change their thinking as well.

I want to ask you a question. How much time have you spent on your phone, Facebook, or other devices this week? How much time have you spent with God? Hmmm ... I thought so. We carry around our phones and watch TV like it's the normal thing to do if we have a spare hour or even just a few minutes. I hate it when I'm out with a friend and he or she is constantly on their phone instead of interacting with me. It's like we've found our new Bible in all the technology junk. If you ask me, that's a little scary.

In the summer of 2012, I worked with a team called Camp at Home. We were a mission team that travelled from church to church bringing camp to kids who couldn't make it to the campgrounds. I loved it. Most of the places I travelled to had no TV, movies, or even good cell phone connections. I learned the hard way how to live without social media and all that technology. When I came home from summer camp, I decided to cut out all TV shows and I stopped listening to secular music. Within a month, my motives and desire for technology had changed. I still watched a good movie once or twice a week, but I didn't live for technology anymore. It felt so good.

Today I get joy out of hearing songs like "Uptown Funk" and "Happy." I also love shows such as *Castle* and *24*, but I have a new approach to the way I view technology. Spending that time away from it all taught me how to enjoy technology but not let it rule my life. I hope you can take an honest look at the way you view technology and change your habits and motives.

So to the girl who's just sitting on the couch—you are worth so much more than the next Netflix binge. You were created for the extraordinary, the top-of-the mountain experiences, and living life to the fullest! None of this is going to happen if you stay in your comfort zone. Yes, change and growth can be hard and painful, but nothing is more painful than staying stuck when you could be out living your dreams!

God wants the very best for us. He wants us to get up every morning with excitement and joy to live out His purpose of love, gratitude, and praise. He wants us to seek Him out and never settle for anything less than the very best. Although I'll always enjoy a good movie from time to time, I know that there's more meaning to my life than simply sitting on the couch ... there has to be.

Just like any good movie, life always has a story line. *You* have the best story to tell. You have a journey unlike any other. You have mistakes, struggles, triumphs, and visions that no one else possesses. There will never be another you. There will never be another girl who has your story, your gifts, or your character—so own it! And get out there and start living that amazing story! Seriously.

We are the daughters of the King of the universe, the King of the world. You were made to shine. You were made to walk in His lightness. You were meant for the extraordinary. You were meant to value your time and spend it well. Life is a gift, so cherish it. It's better than any movie or television show ever made.

A Perspective on Money

God tells us through His Word that our view of money impacts our lifestyle and holy temples. Let's take a look at what God tells us about money: "*Go sell everything you have and give to the poor, and you will have treasure in heaven. Then come, follow me,*" (Mark 10:21); "*Blessed are you who are poor, for yours is the kingdom of God,*" (Luke 6:20); "*... life does not consist in an abundance of possessions,*" (Luke 12:15); "*But seek first the kingdom of God and his righteousness, and all these things will be added to you,*" (Matthew 6:33, ESV).

The kingdom of heaven is like treasure hidden in a field, which a man [or woman] found and covered up. Then in his joy he goes and sells all that he has and buys that field. (Matthew 13:44, ESV)

If you think about it, the money we have really isn't ours. We'll never be able to take any of our possessions or favourite material items with us to heaven; therefore, store up your treasure in heaven. Enjoy what God gives you in this life, but remember to serve God, not the money.

Speak Justice, Love Mercy, and Walk Humbly

He has shown you, O mortal, what is good. And what does the LORD require of you? To act justly and to love mercy and to walk humbly with your God. (Micah 6:8)

God requires all of us to act justly; stand up for your values and live out your beliefs. Learn to say "no," and walk away from the dangers of technology and self-absorption. God requires all of us to love mercy, to tell our family and friends about the love and mercy of Christ Jesus. God requires us all to walk humbly with our God by the way we dress and by what we watch.

Like Seriously

Instead of turning on your TV, strolling through social media, or buying the latest fashion accessory, take a serious look at your life. Here are some tools and steps to help you develop a healthy lifestyle for your holy temples:

1. Take a long walk with God. This could be at a beach or in the woods.

---

2. Turn off all technology for a full twenty-four hours.
3. Do not turn on any technology until you have spent quality time with God.
4. Make sure that what you are watching or what you are hearing are pleasing to God.
5. Make a reality check of your closet.
6. Love the woman in the mirror.
7. Speak justice, love mercy, and walk humbly.
8. Remember that everything you do tells a story of your love for Jesus.

Be Empowered

Don't you know that you yourselves are God's temple and that God's Spirit dwells in your midst? If anyone destroys God's temple, God will destroy that person; for God's temple is sacred, and you together are that temple. (1 Corinthians 3:16–17)

"Dear friend, I pray that you may enjoy good health and that all may go well with you, even as your soul is getting along well," (3 John 1:2).

"Let your roots grow down into him and draw up nourishment from him. See that you go on growing in the Lord, and become strong and vigorous in the truth ... " (Colossians 2:7, TLB).

"Jesus Christ is the same yesterday and today and forever," (Hebrews 13:8).

Thought to Ponder
To the Girl Who Is Living in a "Sexy World"
By: Kathryn Gross

Each day we are being fed messages about how girls and women should be. The world shouts out that all women should be sexy. This message is found in the television shows and movies we watch, the Internet sites we browse, the songs we listen to, the magazines we look through, and even on the billboards we drive by. Most of the world tells us that the ideal woman is hot, or sexy. But these messages aren't what God tells His daughters. Your worth and value isn't based on your body, your clothes, your makeup, or your "sex appeal." The goodness of our physical bodies is expressed in scripture (Genesis 1:27). God took great care when creating us, and Genesis 2:23-25 expresses the goodness of our physical bodies, which God created:

> *The Lord God fashioned into a woman the rib which He had taken from the man, and brought her to the man. The man said, "This is now bone of my bones, and flesh of my flesh; She shall be called Woman, because she was taken out of Man."*
> (Genesis 2:22–23, NASB)

We live in a fallen world where the goodness of creation and relationships has been broken. In our obsession with our bodies and clothing to gain value and acceptance, we make idols of ourselves. We need to realign ourselves with God's values.

> *But the Lord said to Samuel, "Don't judge by his appearance or height, for I have rejected him. The LORD doesn't see things the way you see them. People judge by outward appearance, but the LORD looks at the heart."* (1 Samuel 16:7, NLT)

Be a daughter of the King who seeks to love God with her heart, mind, and body.

chapter five

This Thing Called "Beauty"

To the girl who thinks you're fat because
you're not a size zero. You are a beautiful one.
It is society that is ugly.[9]
MARILYN MONROE

BEAUTY IS DEFINED IN THE DICTIONARY AS A COMBINATION OF qualities, such as shape, colour, form, and sight. It also says that a beautiful person has perfect form and is always pleasing to the eye. *Ugh.* When I read that I cringe. How can I have a perfect form and always be pleasing to every eye? I can't. We can't. The world is simply missing out on a deeper and more meaningful beauty. I know I will never measure up to what the world calls beautiful. I want to share with you the definition of beauty that I've learned through my walk with God.

She is far from perfect, but loves the God who is. She may have scars or a huge nose, but that doesn't matter to her as much as knowing she is loved by her Creator. She praises Him in song, in her words, and in her actions. She doesn't only admire her own beauty, but she looks for the beauty in others too. She is free to be herself, yet she explores all the opportunities God has for her. She doesn't follow the world's standards, but she's able to stand up, different from the rest of the world. She doesn't have all the answers, but she puts her trust in the One who does. She goes on running towards the call God has placed on her, never turning back.

Are you able to forget the world's definition and find it in God instead? I pray and hope you do. I want you to be the girl who runs towards God's grace, knowing your beauty rests in our amazing Lord and Saviour. Yeah!

I'm amazed by how our bodies work. I know I talked about how our bodies need to be a holy temple, but I want to talk a bit deeper here. God designed each of us so differently, yet we have one commonality—Jesus Christ. He saw our unformed body in our mother's womb. He counted all our days, even before they came to be. He knew our hair colour, our skin colour, and our height. No matter how different we may appear on the outside, God loves us all the same. I am so thankful there are no outsiders to His love. So today, believe and know you are loved and beautiful by God's standards.

I want to take some time to talk about my ten natural beauty tips that have helped me remember that my beauty is in Christ.

1. Throw Away the Scale

What is your relationship with your scale? Are you so scared to step on it that you hide it in your closet? Or do you step on it every morning, obsessed with your daily weight? I know our weight matters for most of us. Back in high school there was a period in my life where I let my scale dictate my mood and my perception of my own beauty. It ate away at me. Instead of loving the skin I was in, I became obsessed with the ideal weight. The scary part was that my "ideal weight" was not at all in line with God's weight of love for me.

I'm asking you to throw away the scale and step into God's grace. This isn't easy. It's been about a year since I last weighed myself. Instead,

I weigh myself with God's truth. I literally have positive words, such as, "joyful," "beautiful," "limitless," "powerful," and "love" written on my mirrors, so that instead of being tempted to weigh myself to my own standards, I remind myself of who I truly am. Instead of letting a number dictate my life, I surround myself with godly principles. Since I've thrown my scale away, I feel like a new woman! Candace Cameron Bure, in her book *Reshaping It All*, says:

> God created each one of us in our own unique way. Just like a snowflake we all hold a blueprint that differs one from another. It's great to lose weight and keep our bodies healthy and strong, but it's also important that we appreciate who we are today—with or without extra pounds.[10]

I may be a few extra pounds heavier today than I was when I let the scale rule my life, but I'm more happy, carefree, and bold in who I am. I love my body … all of it. Throwing away your scale may be the best thing that will happen to you regarding your own body image. Never let a number dictate your worth or beauty. Step off the scale, shake those hips, and dance, girl!

2. Yes, Beauty Sleep Works

Sleep is essential, and developing a consistent sleeping pattern will add quality to your life. I believe everyone should be getting eight hours of sleep per night. If you have a consistent sleeping pattern with eight hours of sleep, your body will get rid of stress and hormone imbalances, which will make you feel so much better when you wake up the next morning. When your body is sleeping, it's able to shut down and repair. This will add energy, endurance, and readiness for the next day.

Here are some simple steps to make sure you get a restful night's sleep:

- Turn off all technology one hour before bed.
- Make sure the room has as little light as possible.
- Do not exercise right before you sleep.
- Have some chamomile tea to help calm any stress or nervousness (I prefer hot milk and Ovaltine).
- Don't sleep the whole day away; God has things for you to do, so get up!
- Say a prayer before bed.

3. Start the Day with a Healthy Breakfast

A lot of people get up, rush around, and grab something fast for breakfast. While I know this life can be crazy busy, this is simply not acceptable. Every person needs to start the day with a healthy breakfast. This may mean you get up twenty minutes earlier, but let me tell you, it is definitely worth it.

I used to eat sugary cereal and those amazing cinnamon buns every morning. However, I noticed that by the time 10:00 a.m. rolled around, my stomach was crying for more food. This was because I wasn't starting my day with the proper nutrients. When we eat a lot of sugar and cheap fill, it goes straight through our bodies and makes for a bad morning. Make sure you get up and eat a solid meal of protein to give you energy for the day. Some examples of my kind of a healthy breakfast are:

- omelettes—the best ones are made with feta cheese, ham, veggies, and even some bacon
- oatmeal with flaxseed and almond milk
- eggs and avocado on rye toast
- any type of smoothie
- maybe even chicken

All that being said, I love food! Food is meant to be enjoyed. I'll never say that pigging out on the couch every day is wise or honouring to God, but I want you to enjoy that full piece of cheesecake, that whole large pizza, and still love your body and figure afterwards. And if you ever come visit me at my house, I will prepare for you a brunch with all the fixings! My favourite thing to eat is ice cream. I love it so much that one of my friends and I declared ice cream to be the fifth major food group. Life simply isn't meant to just count the calories. So eat the healthy stuff, but enjoy every bite of that brownie and ice cream.

4. Exercise and Love It!

Exercise is important for our bodies for many reasons. It improves mood, builds muscles, reduces stress, makes you love yourself more, gives you more energy, keeps your immune system healthy, and even helps to postpone aging. The good news is that we don't have to live at a gym or run a marathon. Exercise can start by recognizing our day-to-day activities and making the most of it by staying active and keeping our body moving.

Here's a list of exercising ideas to get your body moving: cleaning (making beds, vacuuming, washing floors), gardening, dancing (in your underwear!), swimming, walking, hiking mountains (my favourite!), biking, skating, running, any type of sport, grocery shopping, and using the stairs.

Here's what happens to our bodies when we exercise regularly:

- Better sleep
- No unnecessary weight gain
- Enhanced muscles
- Increased endurance
- Decreased stress
- More brain cell growth

Exercise is also an act of worship. As we've learned before, our bodies are a holy temple, a holy sacrifice to the Lord. When we take good care of our bodies, we honour God. Here's a list of how to develop a proper fitness habit:

- Write down your goals. Where are you now and where do you want to be six months from now? Keep your goals challenging but also realistic.
- Take small steps. There's nothing worse than having too high of an expectation for yourself and not being able to reach it. Start small and work your way up.
- Don't put too much pressure on yourself. Don't be motivated by your body image, but exercise because you know it honours God.
- Be willing to adapt and rewrite your goals as time goes on.
- Give yourself rewards.
- Keep a chart of what you did and for how long.
- Start at ten minutes a day and gradually work yourself up to at least thirty minutes of exercise per day.
- Exercise three to five times a week.
- Warm up and stretch your muscles before and after you exercise.
- Drink lots of water.
- Enjoy it.

What helps me when I exercise is putting on some music and getting into the beat. Whether I'm hiking a mountain or simply washing the floor, it becomes fun to me and I end up not even realizing I'm exercising and helping my overall health.

After three to four weeks of an exercise routine, you'll feel a change in your body. You'll feel more energized, more motivated, and more prepared to conquer day-to-day challenges. Be good to your body.

5. When Using Makeup ...

The only thing I have to say about makeup is to remember to be yourself. Makeup is fun to bring out your eyes or that beautiful smile, but you must be true to yourself. If you're wearing makeup to cover up who you truly are, then you're on a dangerous road. Love your skin and the face God has already given you. Even try going a few days a week without any makeup at all. There is beauty in the raw and natural. The secret with makeup is to make it look like you really aren't wearing any, so have some fun with makeup, but remember to not let it hide who God has made you to be.

6. Smile

Your smile can change the world. Do you know anyone who can walk into a room and light the whole place up? They have a glow and light about them that affects everyone and creates a chain reaction. A smile gives hope, reassurance, love, peace, joy, and kindness. It gives light in the dark places. It speaks grace over the brokenness. I'm asking you today to let your smile change the world.

I also believe that when you smile you're not only a blessing to the people around you, but also to yourself. Smiles and laughter will lift your own spirit. They will be a testament of your faith. In Proverbs, we read that when we trust in God, we can laugh with confidence and peace about what is next in our lives—even through gloom, despair, and doubt.

I encourage you to have a good, hard, healthy laugh today. Smile at someone who needs some love. Allow yourself to be truly happy and blessed. It's contagious. No one else has your smile, so wear it and start changing your world!

7. Say "No" to Vanity and Get into God's Word

Vanity is defined as self-obsession. A vain woman is self-absorbed, self-admired, selfish, and uninterested in other people's beauty or what God has already given her. I'll be honest with you—I have fallen into the trap of self-absorption and wanting to only admire my own beauty. It's human nature, especially for women. Plus, our world is constantly telling us it's okay to be obsessed with ourselves. Whether we're changing our profile picture on Facebook to get 100 likes or spending $100 on the latest pair of jeans, I think we can all be guilty of letting vanity go to our heads.

With God, you and I know we have a different life to lead than just being concerned with our looks. While you can enjoy smiling, wearing makeup, and loving who you truly are, don't lose sight of the One who is the centre of it all.

How do we say no to vanity and being self-absorbed? By starting the day with God's Word. We can't simply state we're beautiful through God today and do nothing about it tomorrow. Getting into God's Word gives us the daily reminder and strength we need to say "no" to the world's definition of beauty. Getting into God's Word shows us and teaches us the correct way to live. Say "no" to the mirrors, the glamour, and the popularity contests and pick up the Bible.

8. Admire Other People's Beauty

Part of embracing the beauty God has given us is learning to admire other people's beauty without questioning our own. God has created beauty all around us. I see it when the young mother cares for her crying newborn. I see it when my grandma makes sure to save me a piece of her pumpkin pie. I see it when my best friend walks down the aisle on her wedding day. Wouldn't it be great if you and I stopped comparing ourselves to people and embraced their beauty too? How strong we'd become if we stepped off our own stage and encouraged others.

I challenge you to live a life in which you can compliment others for their beauty and what God has given them without letting it defeat you. Have joy when someone reflects God's grace. Rejoice with your sister when she goes off with her prom date.

If I've learned anything through this journey, it's that I need encouragement. Yes, I know I'm pretty, but when someone compliments me—whether about my hair or the good job I did at work—it leaves a mark and impacts my view of myself. This is your chance to speak life into someone else's heart. When you see something beautiful in someone, tell them. It may only take a second, but for them it could last a lifetime.

9. Reflect Your Creator

This is probably the most important point. I talked about God as our beauty mark, but He can only be our beauty mark if we actually let Him. We each are unique. None of us are the same, and that's a beautiful thing. We each have different talents, gifts, and abilities to use to show we are living for God. When we truly live for God, we reflect Him, and our lives become radiant. You'll start walking around this world knowing you have purpose and motivation to press on. And people will look at you and say, "There's something different about that girl." That "something different" is evidence that you love God and reflect Him. Share His love with the girl beside your locker. Go visit that neighbour who's sick. Be kind and honour your parents and family. Speak life into the broken. Lead a life of love because of who God made you to be. I find that words of affirmation really help me to do this. I call these "creative positive statements." They can be scripture verses you put on your walls, a morning prayer, or actual words of affirmation to remind you who you are in Christ. Here are some examples:

"I love the body God gave me."

"Today, I'm going to be me and not compare myself to others."

"Sarah, you are to encourage at least three people today in their walk with God."

"I am beautiful in His sight."

Find ways to help yourself reflect our amazing Creator, and let your beauty become radiant.

10. Own your Imperfections

Every girl has insecurities. Every girl has some type of flaw. Every girl has imperfections. Sometimes I look in the mirror and that's all I see. The imperfections. The flaws.

One day, it finally hit me. What if our imperfections are there to remind us that there's only one person who is perfect? God didn't give us our imperfections to laugh at us or to try to make our lives harder. I believe He gave them to us as a blessing. He's making us humble. Remember that there is purpose behind every fault, limitation, failure, and flaw. I've decided that when I look in the mirror and all I can see are my flaws, I'll thank my Creator. Even though I'm full of flaws, I put my trust in the One who is flawless beyond compare. He is the One who picks up every broken piece to fill me and make me whole. Allow Him to do the same in your life. The next time you think about your major imperfection, ask God to make you humble. And then ask Him to make you whole. He will. Every single time.

Maybe you have a gap in your teeth that you're embarrassed about. Maybe you have a limp when you walk. Maybe you have really frizzy hair. I'll let you in on another one of my secrets—there's no such thing as being perfect. So instead of spending all that time and money on trying to make yourself perfect, embrace how God has already made you. Girl, appreciate that gap in your teeth. Girl, rock your frizzy hair. Girl, own your imperfections.

I know you're a smart girl. I know you can make your own decisions, so be wise. Be mindful. Even though it's God who makes you beautiful, once you know the truth, you are to represent His beauty for the rest of the world to see. There are younger girls who are looking up to you as their role model for beauty. Will you share with them the good news of how God became your beauty mark? Remember that you represent God in everything you do, including how you wear this thing called beauty.

The Beauty Mark of a Godly Woman

SHE SMILES
She smiles because she knows that all things work together for the good of those who love Him, who are called according to His purpose (Romans 8:28).

SHE IS CONFIDENT
She knows her self-worth comes from having her identity in Christ, not from clothing, popularity, or boys.

SHE ENDURES
She endures through the temptations and hard times, because she knows God is bigger than her problems.

SHE REMAINS HUMBLE
She serves God not because she wants to impress others, but because she sincerely loves the Lord.

SHE LOVES
She loves ... truly loves. She doesn't pretend to love, but loves people deeply, because Christ is love.

SHE SPEAKS FAITH
She is clothed with strength and dignity. She laughs without fear of the future, because she knows her God is faithful.

SHE LIVES IN TRUTH
She is grounded in God's Word and lives out His truths.

SHE HOPES
She knows she is not perfect, but she remains strong, knowing she is the daughter of the perfect King.

SHE IS WISE

She thinks before she speaks, and she is always ready to learn more.

SHE IS AN EXAMPLE

She is an example to all those around her, because she is radiant from the inside out.

Be Empowered

Your beauty should not come from outward adornment, such as elaborate hairstyles and the wearing of gold jewelry or fine clothes. Rather, it should be that of your inner self, the unfading beauty of a gentle and quiet spirit, which is of great worth in God's sight. (1 Peter 3:3–4)

"For we are God's handiwork, created in Christ Jesus to do good works, which God prepared in advance for us to do," (Ephesians 2:10).

"The grass withers and the flowers fall, but the word of our God endures forever," (Isaiah 40:8, NIV).

Thought to Ponder

To the Girl Who Has No Earthly Father

By: Sarah Evangeline

I know what it's like to go to bed without having a father to kiss and hug me goodnight. I know what it's like to look for boys to fill the void a father should have filled. I know what it's like to wonder if someone will ever love me like a father should.

At the age of five, I came home from a weekend away to a half-empty house. I saw the panic and sadness sweeping over my mom—*my dad has left*, I thought. I had never been more confused in my life. Why did I have two separate houses? Why would my parents fight and argue? Why didn't I have the normal, perfect family everyone else seemed to have? One day my mom said to me: "Sarah, you have a Father in heaven who will love you no matter what."

Today, I love my dad. He has come and supported me in my basketball games, high school graduation, and birthday celebrations. He even helped me get through my toughest math courses in university; however, it hasn't always been a pretty picture. I remember crying myself to sleep most nights. I remember being an angry and sad little girl with attachment issues. I was broken. I was hurt, even if I hadn't truly realized and dealt with the pain yet. I know my relationship with my dad will always be a struggle because we live in a broken world. A fragile world. A world where divorce happens, even when we try to love and serve God. I love my dad, and I know he loves me in the best way he can. I've also learned that he will never be able to fully satisfy my needs like my Father in heaven does, because no one can. I want you girls to know that I don't blame my dad or mom for any of this. There have been many days that I wished for my parents to get back together, but I know it can't be like that. Life can just simply be messy.

I know some of you have grown up with a caring and loving father. This is the way God intended it to be. I know others haven't even met your earthly father; some of you have met your earthly father, but he walked out. Some of you resent your father because He abused or neglected you, and some of you had an amazing dad but he died. Whatever the case, I want to invite you into the knowledge and truth that God is your heavenly Father.

This side of heaven doesn't always have a happy ending, but God is the One who made my family whole again. When I started to think of God as my Father, my whole world changed for the better. Instead of crying myself to sleep, I talked to God. Instead of wishing my dad could see me at my soccer game, I looked out into the crowd and knew God was watching. When I needed help making career choices, I asked God for wisdom. Paul says: "… *yet for us there is one God, the Father, from whom all things and for whom we exist …*," (1 Corinthians 8:6, ESV).

Remember, our God is perfect; He makes no mistakes. You are to love your earthly father because that's what God commands us to do as His followers, but you have the chance to also love Jesus Christ as your heavenly Father. He will never leave your side.

chapter six

Leave a Legacy of Grace,
Part I

Emotions are indicators, not dictators.
They can indicate where your heart is in
the moment, but that doesn't mean they have
the right to dictate your behavior and boss you
around. You are more than the sum total
of your feelings and perfectly capable of
that little gift...called self-control.[11]
LYSA TERKERUST

THERE'S A SIDE TO ME THAT IS KIND, THOUGHTFUL, ENCOURAGING, AND optimistic. There's also a side of me that can be angry, impatient, and self-centred. I know what it's like to say something positive one minute and be totally impatient and negative the next. I am human, but being human does not give me the excuse to behave this way. I want to do better. I want to use my emotions and words for good. I want to react to situations with love and grace. As Christians, we need to try our best to do this. The psalmist also prayed for the grace to live this way: "*Let the words of my mouth and the meditation of my heart be acceptable in your sight, O LORD, my rock and my redeemer,*" (Psalm 19:14, ESV). God is my rock and my redeemer. I want my words and emotions to be acceptable in His sight. I want to show others my belief in God through speaking life over my words and knowing how to control my emotions.

Life or Death

I've created a chart to illustrate the difference between speaking life and speaking death.

LIFE	DEATH
Tells the truth	Lies are always exposed
Stays calm	Makes cutting remarks
Brings healing	Opens up old wounds
Hard worker	Lazy
Sensible	Unaware & clueless
Joyful	Hateful
Godly	Plotting evil
Saves lives	Despised
Stands firm	A murderous ambush
Self-control	Quick tempered
Wise	Foolish
Peace	Stressed out

The tongue is one of the most powerful tools God gave us. We can choose to let our words breathe life into another person, or we can let our words breathe death. Have you ever thought about how your words and tone of voice can impact those around you? Sometimes words can feel like daggers, and sometimes they can feel like love: "*The tongue can bring death or life; those who love to talk will reap the consequences*," (Proverbs 18:21, NLT).

Any girl can wear the makeup and the pretty dress, but if she's constantly cutting people down with negative and hurtful words, she's not embracing her beauty from the inside, but instead relying on the makeup and clothes to hide what's truly going on inside. True beauty starts from the inside out—the way we talk and control our emotions. Are you going to let your beauty depend on what you wear, or are you going to dig deeper?

James gives us a clear picture of the power of our tongue. Indeed, we all make many mistakes. For if we could control our tongues, we would be perfect and could also control ourselves in every other way. The tongue is a small thing that makes grand speeches. A tiny spark can set a great forest on fire. And the tongue is a flame of fire. It is a whole world of wickedness, corrupting your entire body. Sometimes the tongue can praise our Lord and Father and sometimes it curses those who have been made in the image of God.

Guarding Our Words

I'm going to show you, through God's Word, how we can guard our words and use them to speak life.

"The words of the godly [woman] *are a life-giving fountain,"* (Proverbs 10:11, NLT).

"It is foolish to belittle one's neighbor; a sensible person keeps quiet," (Proverbs 11:12–13, NLT).

"Those who control their tongue will have a long life," (Proverbs 13:3, NLT).

"A truly wise person uses few words; a person with understanding is even-tempered," (Proverbs 17:27, NLT).

"Fools have no interest in understanding; they only want to air their own opinions," (Proverbs 18:2, NLT).

"Watch your tongue and keep your mouth shut, and you will stay out of trouble," (Proverbs 21:23, NLT).

"There is more hope for a fool [who speaks her own words] *than for someone who speaks without thinking,"* (Proverbs 29:20).

What do those verses tell you about guarding your words? To me, God is saying to be careful how I speak. Each word is a gift, and words can have consequences. I want my words to be a life-giving fountain because I learn to think before I speak. Do you see yourself in any of these verses? If so, stop and ask God to help your words to become a life-giving fountain. First Peter 3:8–12 gives us this illustration:

Finally, all of you should be of one mind ... Be tenderhearted and keep a humble attitude. Do not repay evil for evil ... Instead, pay them back with a blessing ... If you want to enjoy life and see many happy days, keep your tongue from speaking evil and your lips from telling lies. Turn away from evil and do good ... The eyes of the Lord watch over those who do right, and his ears are open to their prayers. But the Lord turns His face against those who do evil. (NLT)

Words Direct Our Paths

There's so much power in our words. The way we talk can direct the course of our life. Here are some examples:

The plans of the godly are just; the advice of the wicked is treacherous. The words of the wicked are like a murderous ambush, but the words of the godly save lives. The wicked die and disappear, but the family of the godly stand firm. A sensible person wins admiration, but a warped mind is despised.
(Proverbs 12:5–8, NLT)

The wicked are trapped by their own words, but the godly escape such trouble. Wise words bring many benefits, and hard work brings rewards. Fools think their own way is right, but the wise listen to others. A fool is quick tempered, but a wise person stays calm when insulted. An honest witness tells the truth; a false witness tells lies. Some people make cutting remarks, but the words of the wise bring healing. Truthful words stand the test of time, but lies are soon exposed. Deceit fills hearts that are plotting evil; joy fills hearts that are planting peace! The Lord detests lying lips, but he delights in those who tell the truth.
(Proverbs 12:13–20, 22, NLT)

The Gift of Silence

Have you ever thought about silence as a gift? I wish I could remember this more often when I react to certain situations. Proverbs 21:23 says, "*Watch your tongue and keep your mouth shut and you will stay out of trouble,*" (NLT); "*For by your words you will be acquitted, and by your words you will be condemned,*" (Matthew 12:37).

You and I have the choice to be silent. Just think, if every person on this planet spent more time thinking about what they were going to say, instead of just speaking the first thing that came into their minds, we would have fewer arguments, hurt friendships, and dishonesty. Instead of speaking right away with cutting remarks and a quick-temper, I want to have faith-filled words. I want to think before I speak, so a rude remark can turn into an encouragement, a judgement into praise, and a problem into a solution.

The Issue of Gossip

Gossip is destructive. Gossip is damaging. Gossip is dangerous. Gossip happens when a group of two or more people talk about facts that aren't necessarily true. Paul instructs us in Colossians 4:6 to: "*Let your conversation be always full of grace, seasoned with salt, so that you may know how to answer everyone.*"

Nothing good can come from destroying someone behind their back. If you don't have the courage to say something to their face, why do you talk about them behind their back? Gossip will also destroy friendships, create divisions in families, and possibly impact your school and job. I think back to all the girlfriends I had in high school and realize that the girls I used to gossip with are no longer my friends. The friendships that have lasted are the ones I didn't gossip about. Oh, dear sister, gossip is so displeasing to God. Instead, let your conversations be full of grace. Your words leave a legacy. Like my grandpa says, "You can't do the Lord's work by tearing someone else down." "*A troublemaker plants seeds of strife; gossip separates the best of friends,*" (Proverbs 16:28, NLT). Refusing to gossip is a beautiful thing you can choose to do.

When people start gossiping about you, remember to not let man's words define you. Your true worth is found in Christ alone. The main reason why others are talking about you in a negative way is that they don't understand the truth of being defined by God. But you do, so hold your head up high; God says you are more precious than gold.

Here are some ideas to help you stop gossip:
- Learn to walk away.
- Think before you speak.
- See the positive side to things.
- Demonstrate self-control.

- Terminate gossip as soon as it starts.
- Counteract negative talk with positive words, such as "Yes, Rebecca may walk funny, but she sure has a beautiful smile," or, "Actually, I think Jenny is one of the smartest people in the class."
- Abstain from gossip and you'll start to see a chain reaction.
- Pray. Ask God to help you in these situations.

In a world that thrives on gossip, I encourage you to be the one who lifts people up. Besides, there's no room for gossip if you want to embrace your inner beauty with Christ. Already, you are starting to leave a beautiful legacy of grace.

Negative Self-Talk

The mind is such a powerful thing. It will either give you peace and hope or lead you into darkness. Often we are our own worst enemy. Negative talk fills our minds; we love to judge and put ourselves down. Our voice in our head usually speaks the most negative and most dangerous words. Do any of these thoughts sound familiar?

Ew, Sarah, why on earth do you have another pimple? And right on your lip too! Gross!

You will never get that job, because you just don't have enough experience, so don't even try.

All those girls are staring at me. Oh, it's probably because they don't like my hair or shoes.

I'm just not worth the trouble.

I'm pretty sure you could come up with your own negative self-talk too. We all have negative thoughts about ourselves, but I don't want to live like this … do you?

In order to change our negative self-talk, we have to change our thoughts and heart. We may not have control over certain situations, but we have control over how we think, process, and act on it. Jesus says, "*For out of the abundance of the heart the mouth speaks,*" (Matthew 12:34, ESV).

If you're a judgemental person, you'll have a critical tongue, which means you'll have a critical mind. If you're ungrateful, you'll have a negative mind. If you're loving and see the best in situations, you'll have a loving heart. If you have a faithful heart, you'll be able to speak life in the midst of chaos. Do you see how the mind and heart have an effect on your words? We have to train our mind and heart towards the positive and looking for the best outcomes rather than the negativity and believing the worst.

How to train our mind and heart:

1. Stay focused on Jesus. You must spend time in His Word, understanding His character, and praying for guidance and strength. You can't change your thoughts and tongue overnight, and you can't do it alone. Before you get out of bed in the morning, ask God to help your mind and heart.

2. Have an accountability buddy. Sometimes I wish I could be more like my mom. She has grace and kindness woven into her mind and words in ways I may never understand. She finds laughter in the midst of chaos, and she always knows how to see the positive side of things. I honestly don't know what I would have done if I hadn't grown up with a mother who does everything she can to believe in people and spur them on. Who do you have in your life who you can count on to help you see the positive side of things? Find someone who can encourage and believe in you to help you get rid of all that negative talk.

3. As soon as that negative thought comes into your mind, change your thinking. When you notice your mind going towards the negative, start singing a song, or say out loud, "God's way,

God's way, God's way." Whatever you do, be in control of your emotions and words.

4. Do not give up. These strategies could take weeks, months, or even a year. Keep it up, because you deserve to live a better life.

Be Empowered

"But letting the Spirit control your mind leads to life and peace," (Romans 8:6b, NLT).

"I have hidden your word in my heart, that I might not sin against you," (Psalm 119:11, NLT).

"… keep these desires and thoughts in the hearts of your people forever, and keep their hearts loyal to you," (1 Chronicles 29:18).

"Be strong in the Lord and in his mighty power," (Ephesians 6:10, NLT).

"And we all, who with unveiled faces contemplate the Lord's glory, are being transformed into his image with ever-increasing glory, which comes from the Lord who is the Spirit," (2 Corinthians 6:18).

Thought to Ponder

To the Girl Who May Have Forgotten God's Amazing Promise for Us All

By: Sarah Evangeline

I was the little girl who was always fascinated by rainbows. After a rainy day, I would go and look for them in the sky. I also saw them in the waterfalls and creeks as I hiked. I mean, it is pretty amazing how colours like that can just form and look so magnificent, right?

Of course, I was told the story of Noah in Sunday school. After the flood had dried up, God sent a sign to promise that He would never flood the earth again. It wasn't just a sign—it was a promise.

A promise that would last forever.

Late one night, I started reading the book of Genesis. I came once again to the story of Noah and God confirming this kind of promise. Scripture says:

> *I have placed my rainbow in the clouds. It is the sign of my covenant with you and with all the earth. When I send clouds over the earth, the rainbow will appear in the clouds, and I will remember my covenant with you and with all living creatures. Never again will the floodwaters destroy all life. When I see the rainbow in the clouds, I will remember the eternal covenant* [promise] *between God and every living creature on the earth.* (Genesis 9:13–16)

Can you believe it?

Every single time a rainbow comes into the sky, not only do we see it, but God sees it and thinks of you and me. He remembers the promise He made thousands and thousands of years ago.

So wherever you are this week, know that all things work together for the good of those who love Him. And next time there is a storm, look up. Look up into the sky and remember the promise.

The promise that lasts forever.

chapter seven

Leave a Legacy of Grace,
Part II

Whatever God is urging you to clear away cannot
begin to be compared to what he ultimately
wants to bring you.[12]
BETH MOORE

GOD IS SUCH AN AMAZING GOD FOR MAKING US INTO INTERESTING beings that acquire such emotions. Emotions mean "to move," literally meaning that emotions move you. Emotions are a good thing. They can send a signal; they can tell us when something is going wrong and to pay attention. Emotions are great connectors. When you're in love or when you're helping a friend, your emotions help you to relate to others in a deep and meaningful way. Emotions can help you solve problems. All in all, God meant for feelings and emotions to be felt. Listen to your emotions and value them.

On the other hand, if we act out our emotions in a negative way, they can be hurtful to others, so we need to be careful and conscious of this. Do your emotions hurt others? Are your emotions controlling you, or are you controlling them? Do emotions dictate your actions?

You don't have to be a victim of your emotions or be controlled by them. By trusting in God and not our feelings, we can bring our emotions back on track and into a healthy light. Feelings come and go, but God remains the same.

It's time to take control of your emotions. James 1:19 tells us how we are to react to situations: "*Everyone should be quick to listen, slow to speak and slow to become angry*." One of my biggest weaknesses is that I try to do everything in my own strength. I've learned that this can lead to doubt, worry, stress, and, eventually, negative thoughts and words.

How we react to situations shows how well we know Jesus. How is your relationship with God? Do you see how it affects your reactions to situations and people? Do you get angry and impatient every time something doesn't go your way? Do you think before you speak, remaining patient and calm? Here are some of the emotions I came up with that I deal with on a day-to-day basis. I've left some blanks for you to fill in if you wish.

Happy	Joyful	Laughter
Anger	Sadness	Jealousy
Scared	Fearful	Excited
Worried	Insecure	Ashamed
Regret	Guilt	Naggy

God gave us emotions for a reason. Expressing our emotions honours God, but there is a certain time for them.

Let's talk about one of the biggest emotions: anger. Anger is meant to be felt. We see anger in King David in the book of Psalms. King David wrote beautiful poems of praise, but also psalms in which he was angry and challenging God. We see anger in Queen Esther when she worried about going to the king to save her people. We see anger in Moses when he led the people out of Egypt. Paul says this about anger:

... don't sin by letting anger control you. Don't let the sun go down when you are still angry, for anger gives a foothold to the devil ... let everything you say be good and helpful, so that your words will be an encouragement to those who hear them. (Ephesians 4:26, 29, NLT)

Scripture also admonishes us, "*Do not repay evil with evil ...,*" (1 Peter 3:9).

Anger can motivate us to take action against poverty and stand up for our values and beliefs. It can help us solve problems and release stress; however, God warns us that anger can hurt others and control us if we aren't careful. If you have a conflict with someone and you're angry, you need to express that anger in a healthy way and deal with the issue. When we allow our anger to hurt someone, perhaps by hitting them or telling them they're worthless, we are using unhealthy anger. Healthy anger manifests when someone is getting bullied at school and you stand up for them. Healthy anger shows compassion for people who suffer from natural disasters. Trust God with your anger. You're allowed to freak out. You're allowed to scream and be mad at the world, but you are not allowed to hurt others too.

Negative emotions are also manifested in complaining and arguing, which hurt others.

Do everything without complaining and arguing, so that no one can criticize you. Live clean, innocent lives as children of God, shining like bright lights in a world full of crooked and perverse people. Hold firmly to the word of life. (Philippians 2:14–16, NLT)

Have you ever thought about how your nagging and whining can impact your life? Scripture states: "*It is better to live in a desert land than with a quarrelsome and fretful woman,*" (Proverbs 21:19, ESV). Read the following verses and think about what they say regarding swearing and cursing.

"You must not misuse the name of the Lord your God," (Deuteronomy 5:11, NLT).

"Avoid all perverse talk; stay away from corrupt speech," (Proverbs 4:24, NLT).

"But now is the time to get rid of anger, rage, malicious behavior, slander, and dirty language," (Colossians 3:8, NLT).

Sometimes shame, guilt, and regret creep into our minds. Perhaps we can't let go of past regrets so they affect our future emotions and words. Throughout my life, I've learned that these feelings are only lies that hurt my relationship with God. As soon as I ask God for forgiveness, He takes everything from my past away. I know that with God we are a new creation … so how do we get rid of these feelings? Paul teaches that: "… *anyone who belongs to Christ has become a new person. The old life is gone; a new life has begun,*" (2 Corinthians 5:17, NLT).

Rejoice, ladies! We don't have to live with the lies of shame, guilt, and regret. Leave them at the cross; arise in your new creation. You are never beyond repair; God will meet you exactly where you are.

Put on your new nature, and be renewed as you learn to know your Creator and become like him ... clothe yourselves with tenderhearted mercy, kindness, humility, gentleness, and patience ... Above all, clothe yourselves with love, which binds us all together in perfect harmony ... And always be thankful. (Colossians 3:10, 12, 14–15, NLT)

I'd rather have a grateful and thankful heart and turn my whining and complaining into something godly and beautiful: "... *give thanks in all circumstances; for this is the will of God in Christ Jesus for you,*" (1 Thessalonians 4:18, ESV). Wow, we're to give thanks in all circumstances. Every day we get to choose how we express these emotions. How do you want your emotions to tell your story?

Rise Above It

Last night I had a meltdown. I don't mean I was just crying and eating a gallon of ice cream. I mean I had the hugest meltdown of my life, and my family and two friends witnessed the whole thing. I was crying, yelling, and exploding—all of the worst possible emotions I could feel (yeah, not my brightest moment). This life just seems so hard, busy, and impossible for me right now. This week alone I have two final exams, two final papers to write, this book to get to the editors, and my first day of training for my new job tomorrow. Plus, I need to make supper and do laundry. I'm just so tired and worn out. After letting all my emotions build up inside, I finally had to let them loose, which is why I had the meltdown in the first place.

Today, I want you to know it's okay for you to have bad days, make mistakes, have some regrets, and experience those big meltdowns. If you think every day is supposed to be sparkly, bright, and perfect, you're living in a fantasy world.

The hard times and struggles will come; however, we can choose how we're going to deal with the struggle. Are we going to let it defeat us, or are we going to rise above the struggle? The best way to rise above the challenges of this life is to give them up to God and remember His truths. John 10:10 says, "*I have come that they may have life, and have it to the full.*"

God is bigger than my problems, and with Him, I can handle anything. Just think for a second—God is our heavenly Father. He watches over us. Oh, how it must hurt Him to see us struggle and hurt all on our own. He urges you and I to cry out to Him through our struggles and pain. I also believe there's purpose to every situation, even in our meltdowns. God uses hard times to mold us and shape us. If life was easy, we wouldn't learn anything. We wouldn't grow to our full potential. How can our faith grow or be evident in our lives if we're stuck in a safe and sheltered box? I hope I can bring you peace and encouragement as you go through your next hard time or meltdown. Remember that there is purpose behind the struggle, and remember to rely on God, knowing He brings purpose and gives life to everything. So do not be ashamed of your next meltdown ... just know to rise above it.

My God Is Bigger Than My Problems
Here are some verses to keep in mind as you go through those bad days:

... I tell you not to worry about everyday life—whether you have enough food or drink, or enough clothes to wear ... Can all your worries add a single moment to your life? ... your heavenly Father already knows all your needs. (Matthew 6:25, 27, 32, NLT)

I look up to the mountains—does my help come from there? My help comes from the Lord, who made heaven and earth! He will not let you stumble ... (Psalm 121:1–3)

... when troubles of any kind come your way, consider it an opportunity of great joy. For you know that when your faith is tested, your endurance has a change to grow. (James 1:2)

For our present troubles are small and won't last very long. So we do not look at the troubles we can see, rather we fix our eyes on things that we cannot see— eternal life.

How Is the Stress in Your Life?

Stress comes in all shapes and forms and seems to be the one thing we can never escape. Stress is defined as the feeling of being under too much pressure. Stress is both external and internal.

EXTERNAL PRESSURES OF STRESS:	INTERNAL PRESSURES OF STRESS:
-Having to complete homework	- Negative and judgemental thoughts about yourself and others
-Travelling to work or a social event	-Negative thoughts about the world around you
-Emails, phone calls, or other communication	-Low self-esteem
-Taking care of your family	-Low self-compassion
-Taking care of yourself	-Wanting perfection
-Managing someone's illness	-Discomfort or pain in your body
-Lacking money	-Difficult emotions such as depression, anxiety, guilt, or anger

Stress can be good and bad for your health. Studies have proven that short bursts of stress benefit body function. If you're a little nervous before a test, soccer game, or speech, good stressors go into action and help you do well. I love being a little nervous before I speak, because that actually helps me remember what I have to say. This is called short-term stress. Another example of short-term stress is the type you experience on a roller coaster ride. If you look forward to a ride like this, you feel positive about the stress. However, a lot of stressors can be bad and hinder our whole body. This is called long-term stress, and it needs to be dealt with.

"Getting Rid of Stress" Techniques

These are stress-relieving techniques developed by Lorna Vanderhaeghe[13] and myself. Her techniques have been an influence in my life, and I want to share them with you.

- Breathe: Several times a day, breathe in through your nose and fill your lungs with air until your abdomen rises. Then slowly exhale from your mouth until your lungs are empty. Repeat seven times. I've found this to be helpful even when I'm having trouble falling asleep at night. I lie on my back and repeat this exercise seven times in a row. This helps calm my body and prepares me for all the tasks I know I have the next day.
- Learn the word "no" when you know you have too much on your schedule.
- Learn to take time for yourself. I set a date for myself once a week. I go for a nature walk, watch a movie, or just read a book. But it's me time. Time for me to do what I want and not have anyone bother me. I've learned that this is very beneficial for dealing with stress and anxiety.
- Eat vegetables every day.
- Smile and be positive.

- Believe in yourself.
- Love your family and friends and put them before yourself.
- Talk positive self-talk throughout your day.
- Have positive images and scripture verses on your mirrors and walls to remind yourself of where true worth comes from.
- Stay away from negative people and have a good support system.
- Reduce your "to do" list.
- Manage your time properly.
- Find a solution instead of dwelling on the problem.
- Set boundaries for yourself.
- Let go of grudges and anger.
- Lower your standards for yourself.
- Watch something funny that makes you laugh deep down to your core.
- Dance in your underwear.
- Have a regular sleep pattern. Make sure you're getting eight hours of sleep per night.
- Go for a body massage.
- Start the day with God.
- Think before you speak and act.
- Always have room to grow and do better.

What Does God Say About Stress?

Many of us don't handle stress well. For me, stress seems to come up every day. I stress about the littlest of things. I worry about tomorrow's problems even before I know they're problems. I gave you a huge list of techniques to get rid of stress. The best way to get rid of stress is a combination of proper eating, regular exercise, and the surrender of everything to God. He is the Author of taking our burdens and helping us deal with stress. Jesus says:

Look at the birds of the air; they do not sow or reap or store away in barns, and yet your heavenly Father feeds them ... So do not worry, saying, "What shall we eat?" or "What shall we drink?" or "What shall we wear?" ... But seek first his kingdom and his righteousness, and all these things will be given to you as well. Therefore do not worry about tomorrow. (Matthew 6:26, 31, 33–34a)

You and I can decide to trust in God and let Him take our burdens and worries: "*Do not be anxious about anything, but in every situation, by prayer and petition, with thanksgiving, present your requests to God,*" (Philippians 4:6); "*So don't worry about tomorrow, for tomorrow will bring its own worries,*" (Matthew 6:34, NLT).

God instructs us to pray more, worry less; trust more, worry less; seek God more, worry less. I hope you can give up your burdens and worries to God and decide to trust in Him instead. Psalm 94:19 gives us this truth: "*When doubts* [and worry] *filled my mind, your comfort gave me renewed hope and cheer,*" (NLT).

Change Your Perspective

I'm a drama queen. I'm self-centered. I'm a mess, and so are you. If we're honest with ourselves, we know that we all have two sides to us. For instance, I'm an exploder. I have to talk everything out before I make a decision. This means I talk out the good and the bad before I come to a conclusion. When an impossible situation arises, I can explode every possible outcome, but I've learned that exploding in this way only hurts the people I'm with. Sometimes we're so consumed with ourselves we don't realize that our words and emotions are hurting those around us. Selfishness is defined as concentrating on one's own advantage, pleasure, or well-being without regard for others. Sure, getting our own way can feel good for a moment, but it can leave behind a road of destruction. God commands us in His Word to treat others the way we want to be treated.

I had the opportunity to go to San Diego, California for an internship. God designed the whole experience by opening doors and setting everything in motion. I fell in love with the city and the people of El Cajon, Salvation Army church. I worked with many different people and many different situations. One lady I worked with was named Susan. Every day I saw her working hard in the kitchen and the gardens and making sure everyone else was okay. It wasn't until a few weeks into my internship that I learned she had stage four cancer. I was shocked. Susan was in pain every moment of the day, yet she never complained or stopped working hard. She always saw the positive side of things. She had a different perspective for living, and I wanted it too. Susan showed me how to live a life of love:

> *Watch what God does, and then you do it, like children who learn proper behavior from their parents. Mostly what God does is love you. Keep company with Him and learn a life of love. Observe how Christ loved us. His love was not cautious but extravagant. He didn't love in order to get something from us but to give everything of himself to us. Love like that.* (Ephesians 5:1–2, MSG).

Laughter Is the Best Medicine

"*A cheerful heart is good medicine, but a broken spirit saps a person's strength,*" (Proverbs 17:22, NLT). What does it mean to have a cheerful heart? It doesn't mean that we never have problems or trials, but that we see our problems and situations with a joyful and positive perspective. Let's be real for a second—complaining about something isn't going to change the circumstances. It's your choice—complain and feel worse about the problem, or look at the positive side and have a cheerful heart. Remember to leave behind a fragrance of grace and wisdom. A cheerful heart trusts God with all the outcomes and has faith in what is unseen.

The best advice I can give you is to learn how to laugh. When you make a mistake, instead of responding with frustration and anger, laugh it off. When you're out with your girlfriends, make sure to laugh deep down to your core. And on the loneliest of days, remember that the best is yet to come.

The Fragrance of Abigail

Abigail was one of the wisest and most humble women in the Bible. She spent her life speaking truth and remaining calm in hard circumstances. She was generous, wise, and a great peacemaker. Her joy was found in God, who saves lives. I encourage you to open your Bibles to 1 Samuel 25 to experience this beautiful fragrance as Abigail choses life over death. I will summarize it here for you:

Abigail was married to Nabal, who was a disgrace to her and to his country. He hadn't noticed that King David and his men had been protecting his shepherds. When David's camp started to run out of food, David sent ten messengers to Nabal. The messengers told Nabal that they'd been protecting his shepherds and asked for provisions, but Nabal refused them. He even screamed. Nabal's actions deeply insulted David, who responded by preparing to murder him. A servant told Abigail that Nabal has insulted David and informed her of the danger they now faced.

Abigail was not just intelligent and beautiful, but she was also brave and bold. It would have been easy to let David kill her mean and abusive husband, yet Abigail approached David and, with great diplomacy, humbly offered him a "peace offering." She gave David and his men plenty of food. Her actions, patience, and trust in the Lord saved David from taking a life—one that was only God's to take. The next day, Abigail told Nabal everything that she had done. Thankfully, God spared her from Nabal's wrath. Nabal immediately had a heart attack and ten days later died from heart failure. David remembered Abigail. After Nabal's death, he lost no time asking her to become his wife.

Can you imagine being Abigail and reacting in that way? Nabal was a man of greed, selfishness, and foolishness. Abigail was a woman who possessed true humility, faith, generosity, and wisdom. Rather than letting King David and his men kill Nabal, her words of God's truth saved lives that day. Abigail was not fearful; she reminded King David that Nabal's life was in God's hands, not his. Who could forget someone who leaves a fragrance of wisdom, kindness, and love like Abigail? Paul says, "*Our lives are a Christ-like fragrance, rising up to God*," (2 Corinthians 2:15, NLT).

Abigail lived her life choosing to be a Christ-like fragrance in her emotions, reactions, and words. I want to leave behind that same kind of fragrance wherever I go. I hope you will too.

Be Empowered

"Let any one of you who is without sin be the first to throw a stone at her," (John 8:7).

I appeal to you, brothers and sisters, in the name of the Lord Jesus Christ, that all of you agree with one another in what you say and that there be no divisions among you, but that you be perfectly united in mind and thought. (1 Corinthians 1:10)

"Keep your conscience clear. Then if people speak against you, they will be ashamed when they see what a good life you live because you belong to Christ," (1 Peter 3:16, NLT).

"The Lord detests lying lips, but he delights in those who tell the truth," (Proverbs 12:22, NLT).

"Do to others as you would have them do to you," (Luke 6:31).

"He will wipe every tear from their eyes. There will be no more death or mourning or crying or pain," (Revelations 21:4).

Thought to Ponder
To the Girl Who Wants to Start a Chain Reaction
By: Sarah Evangeline

"But the fruit of the Spirit is love, joy, peace, forbearance, kindness, goodness, faithfulness, gentleness, and self-control," (Galatians 5:22).

The fruit is in our action. As the saying goes, "They will know we are Christians by our love." I believe our lives need to be more profound than just love. I believe people will know we are Christians by our fruit.

It's probably impossible to be all the fruit of the Spirit at one time, right? How can one be filled with love, joy, peace, and gentleness and have self-control all at the same time? Again, this is something you will have to work on and work on and work on until it becomes a natural part of your character.

Fruit takes time to ripen; therefore, you need to allow time to ripen your fruit. This will happen as you grow in your relationship with God and use your words and emotions to bring life. The fruit will also ripen as you practice surrender, solitude, and silence. The fruit will ripen as you endure temptations and hard times. In every part of your life, allow the fruit to ripen so you can allow it to influence all areas.

Living out the fruit of the Spirit may be one of the biggest challenges we face. God doesn't expect us to conquer all of these actions every single moment. God does expect us to try our best and practice these actions as much as we can. It's better to be kind than right. I've learned the hard way to let compassion, love, kindness, peace, and all the fruit of the Spirit lead.

When I was in Spain, I fell in love with the culture and lifestyle. Everyone was relaxed, the food was excellent, and the ocean was only a minute away. It was so peaceful that I forgot for a while that I was supposed to be living for God. One night on my way back to my hotel room, I walked by a homeless man. I've seen a lot of homeless people in my life, but never like this man. He had no kneecaps. Instead, his legs were bent inward, not allowing him to walk or sit. He just stood there smiling at me and wishing people a good day. I looked down and continued walking. I soon thought of Jesus and how He spent most of His life walking the streets of this world telling everyone about the love of God. He didn't have a place to sleep at night or a place to wash his feet. Oh, how self-righteous I thought I was! How dare I! This man, even though I knew nothing about him, inspired me. As he smiled at people walking by, he was ripening his fruit. He couldn't even walk, sit, run, or jump, but he expressed kindness, compassion, gentleness, and love. I want to make my fruit ripen in this way.

Here is a secret: Once you start making the fruit of the Spirit a part of your life, it will become a chain reaction. It will affect all aspects of your life, and people will start to be influenced by you. Proverbs 3:3 says, "*Do not let kindness and truth leave you; bind them around your neck, write them on the tablet of your heart*," (NASB).

Will you let your fruit start to ripen today?

chapter eight

Escape the Bondage
of Living for People's Expectations

*Never hide behind
the fact that you are a woman.*
DR. QUINN: MEDICINE WOMAN

LIVING ACCORDING TO OTHER PEOPLE'S EXPECTATIONS CAN BECOME addictive and toxic. I know this because I've fallen into that trap and have let living for people's approval rule my life. I was living in bondage—a prison from which I could not escape. It was only when I let go of people and this world and held onto God, and God alone, that I was free. Free. It never felt so good. I want to share with you my story, and I hope you too can escape the bondage of living for people's expectations: "[I do not want] *to win the approval of people, but of God. If pleasing people were my goal, I would not be Christ's servant,*" (Galatians 1:10, NLT).

I love spending time with friends and family. I love laughing, dancing, cooking, and even having an honest conversation with them. Unfortunately, there was a time in my life when I got so sucked into caring too much about what others said and thought of me, that I forgot who and what I was living for. I lived to please; I only did things to be noticed and admired.

People are meant for good. God created us in His own image and made us for fellowship and community. People are not the enemy, but how we choose to handle situations can become the enemy. We all care about what other people think of us, but we don't have to live up to their standards or expectations. We're only human. We all make mistakes, have weaknesses, and forget to put God first. *Isn't it okay to live this way*? No. God made us to live for higher standards. He made us to rise above the brokenness of this world and choose Him instead. Some days I don't even know why I deserve His second chances and grace, but I guess the whole point is that we don't deserve it. He gives it away freely. Shouldn't I honour Him with all I have by the way I live my life?

It was when I started to ask myself the big questions that I realized the truth that would set me free: I don't have to live to please other people. It's impossible to please every person, but it is possible to please God, because I already have Him. I don't have to win His attention or love. He gives it freely with no limits; He gives only grace, mercy, discipline, and eternal life. I had to choose between people and God. I decided to choose God.

We all love social media and being with friends, but when we put these things above God, they can become dangerous and lethal. We all care about how many "likes" we have on our Facebook and Instagram photos, so let's stop denying it … okay? I love Facebook and Instagram, because it brings me joy to stay in touch with long-distance friends and to see what my family and friends are up to. But I have a choice to make—will social media hinder or help my relationship with God? I have learned that sometimes my friends and family are worth more than a Facebook status or picture.

It's easy to smile when we walk through the doors of our church. *Everything is fine*. What a lie. Isn't it easy to go to all the right church events, participate in church fundraisers, and even lead Sunday school once in a while? Eventually I had to ask myself if I was doing these things for God's glory, or to impress the people in my church. I realized that sometimes I was only doing these things because I knew it was expected of me. Two years ago, I was left burnt out on my bathroom floor, wanting to stop everything church-related because I finally realized I'd been doing it for other people, not for God. I was hungover living for people's expectations, once again. I realized everything I was doing had become worthless, as I was only more tired and exhausted trying to measure up to everyone's standards. Since then I've learned that when I only live for God's glory, He gives me the strength and wisdom I need.

There are so many lies that I believed when I tried to live up to people's expectations. The lie I struggled with the most was that I could only serve God within the four walls of a church building. That is so biblically incorrect. I have learned that I need to serve God outside the church, not just on Sundays or at a special event. While we need pastors, missionaries, and Sunday school teachers, we also need nurses, stay-at-home-mothers, retail store managers, counsellors, and a friendly neighbour. I've learned that if I could have my way, I would knock down the four walls and never look back.

I think about all the times I acted in kindness just to be acknowledged and respected. Isn't it the greatest feeling in the world when someone thanks us publicly for doing an act of kindness? I used to think so. Eventually that feeling faded, because acts of kindness and generosity should be a natural characteristic of who we are, not ploys for the response and acknowledgement. Am I right? I've learned that I find more peace and grace when I do things anonymously and only for the audience of the One who matters most.

It's so easy to say all the right things and not mean any of it. I think back to all the times I was asked to give my testimony or to pray at a youth retreat. Wow ... so many empty words with so little action. I became so focused on how good my prayer sounded that I asked myself if I was even praying to God anymore? I believe God hears every prayer, and there is never a wrong prayer, but it can be easy to talk without living the walk. There's something beautiful about solitude and bringing it to God before bringing it to people.

Finally, I believe that living in the bondage of people's expectations can turn into self-glory. If we're honest, we love to please ourselves. We're the ones who love the attention, the applause, and the credit. I remember when I was living on my own stage, only to feel the ground beneath me crumbling. And oh, that is the worst way to live. I've learned that I cannot put this expectation onto other people. My goal is to help others follow Christ, not me.

I'm not saying that we have to stop interacting with others, stop praying, or stop attending church. This isn't an excuse for any of those things. What matters is our motives and attitudes. Are we doing it for God's glory, or for people's expectations? We all have the choice to make.

> *For great is the Lord and most worthy of praise; he is to be feared above all gods. For all the gods of the nations are idols, but the Lord made the heavens. Splendor and majesty are before him; strength and glory are in his sanctuary. Ascribe to the Lord, all you families of nations … bring an offering and come into his courts. Worship the Lord in the splendor of his holiness; tremble before him, all the earth.* (Psalm 96:4–9)

We may be rejected by man, but we are accepted and unconditionally loved by the Creator of everything. Who can stand against us?

When we choose God over people's expectations, we're not living for this world, but for eternity. God loves all of us. He made us to love each other too. People can help us with our relationship with God in so many ways. I'm still going to love my church, Facebook, and my friends—I just love my God more. I'm also clothed with different attitudes and motives. I have decided that I am not going to let others dictate my life, but I will own my decisions.

At the end of the day, I don't want to be a follower of other Christians; I want to follow God. Him alone. Period. "*No one can serve two masters. Either you will hate the one and love the other, or you will be devoted to the one and despise the other*," (Matthew 6:24). I choose God. And I am free.

Become Boundless

When was the last time you did something only for the audience of God? When was the last time you made a decision that wasn't based on how many likes you received on Facebook? When was the last time you did something for yourself without feeling guilty? Being addicted to approval means you're always performing, which results in the overwhelming feeling of always needing to be liked and accepted by others. Are you living on your own stage? Are you obsessed with applause and praise? Watch out—you could be on your way to leaving God in the dust.

Here's a description of a woman addicted to approval:
- She will do anything to be accepted.
- She is always trying to measure up to people's standards.
- She changes personality depending on who she is with.
- She is easily offended.
- She does not know her identity is in Christ alone.
- She thinks she is always failing.
- She believes her worth is based on *doing* rather than *being*.
- She is always worried about making other people happy.
- She forgets about her own needs.
- She has trouble making her own decisions.

Can you identify with any of these feelings? I know I can, and, man, is it hard to escape them ... but I have escaped. One of my secrets is that I know God's power is made perfect in my weaknesses: "'*My grace is sufficient for you, for my power is made perfect in weakness.' Therefore I will boast all the more gladly about my weaknesses, so that Christ's power may rest on me*," (2 Corinthians 12:9).

Maybe it's time you got real with God. Maybe it's time you pour your heart out to Him and ask Him to free you from the bondage of approval. Here are some tips for breaking that bondage:

1. Look to God before you look to other people. Remember that your identity rests in God alone. You already have God; you don't need to win His attention or love. He holds your whole life, so look to Him.

2. Learn the word "no." Yes, I've escaped the bondage, but I still deal with people's expectations every day. I just know that I have the power to say "no" when things get too overwhelming, or when I start to feel the world's standards weighing in. You have the choice too. Learn the word "no" and you'll see the beauty it brings to your life.

3. Don't allow man's words to define you. People are always going to be people. People are always going to talk, and they're always going to try to cut you down. You belong to God, so let go of people's criticisms.

4. Practice positive self-talk. This is where the memorization of scripture will come in handy. Any time you feel overwhelmed with the need to measure up to the world's standards, recite a verse that proves your worth lies in Christ.

5. Be yourself and love it. If you're trying to live for people's approval, you leave yourself behind. Remember, there is no one else like you, and no one else can live out your story. So be you and love it.

6. Be kind to yourself.

7. Know your values and morals so that you can stand up for yourself.

8. Remember that people are not the problem, but the way we view them can be. Be kind to others and spend time with them, but know how to take time for yourself too.

9. Help others who are addicted to living for people's expectations. Show them how they too can be free in Christ.

A Quieter Life

Make it your goal to live a quiet life, minding your own business and working with your hands… then people who are not believers will respect the way you live, and you will not need to depend on others. (1 Thessalonians 4:11–12, NLT)

God broke through to me when I read this scripture passage. You see, for a while I was unaware I was even in this kind of bondage. To the outside world, my life looked good and happy, but I was slowly dying on the inside. It wasn't until someone close to me said, "Sarah, you have a problem. You're always caring about what others think of you. When was the last time you did something for yourself? You need to give yourself a reality check."

To my dismay, I discovered that I'd been imprisoning myself to approval. I used to think it was a sin if I did something for myself. I lived in guilt and shame, because I thought if I did something for myself, I couldn't make other people happy. Oh girls, I was so blinded! I was so lost! I was so busy pleasing others and caught up in who I was not that I became undisciplined and wild, spending most of my time running around trying to solve everyone else's problems. I praise the Lord today that I am free, and I pray I never go back.

I have shown you what happens when we are in bondage and how we can escape. Now let's look at a woman who's free from this kind of bondage:

- She knows she is chosen by God.
- She is more concerned about her relationship with God than other people's standards.
- She knows who she is and loves who God created her to be!
- She is able to let go of criticism, because she knows only God defines her.
- She presses on in victory and joy.
- She believes her worth is based on following and knowing Christ.
- She still cares for others, but knows how to meet her own needs.
- She knows her values and can stand up for who she is.
- She is able to enjoy the life God designed her to have.
- She has true freedom.

Freedom in Christ

Christ has set us free; we no longer have to live in the bondage of people or their expectations. Take a look at what Paul writes in Galatians:

Christ has truly set us free. Now make sure that you stay free, and don't get tied up again in slavery… For you have been called to live in freedom … but don't use your freedom to satisfy your sinful nature. Instead, use your freedom to serve one another in love … let the Holy Spirit guide your lives. (Galatians 5:1, 13, 16, NLT)

"For the Lord is the Spirit, and wherever the Spirit of the Lord is, there is freedom," (2 Corinthians 3:17, NLT). Freedom in Christ doesn't mean we get to do whatever we want; it means that we abide

by the Holy Spirit and have freedom from the bondage of our sinful nature. Stand firm in freedom, for you are no longer a slave.

Live for the Audience of the One

As I mentioned above, one the greatest things I learned through all of this was that there is more peace and grace found when I do things anonymously for the audience of the One who matters most. The key to living this way is that I must decrease and God must increase: "*True humility and fear of the Lord lead to riches, honor, and long life*," (Proverbs 22:4, NLT); "*Put on your new nature, and be renewed as you learn to know your Creator and become like him*," (Colossians 3:10, NLT); "*It is foolish to belittle one's neighbor; a sensible person keeps quiet*," (Proverbs 11:12, NLT); "*The Lord supports the humble, but He brings the wicked down into the dust*," (Psalms 147:6, NLT); "*He must become greater and greater, and I must become less and less*," (John 3:30, NLT).

God is inviting you today to let go of living for people and to hold on to Him alone. He offers you freedom in His arms and grace for a better tomorrow. I hope you've been inspired and encouraged to leave that old past behind and start to live for the audience of the One—the One who matters most.

Doing Versus Being

This world teaches us that it is more important to "do" something for God rather than "be" who God already created us to be. From Scripture, we see that God desires us to *do less* and *be more*.

DOING:

1. She is busy in the world—You might be at all the right church events and even plan a ministry, but if

you are too busy and do not rely on the Holy Spirit to guide you, it can become dangerous.

2. She has selfish and exterior motives—We do things to try to impress rather than serve.
3. The things she used to love and enjoy become a chore.
4. She forgets to make time for people and give them her attention.
5. She becomes obsessed with a "to do" list.
6. She relies on her own strength instead of trusting in the God who has no limits.

BEING:

1. She knows how to rest in God's grace and peace.
2. She lives for the audience of One and the rest does not matter.
3. She lives out God's purpose, not her own purpose.
4. She abides in God's love and lets Him go before her.
5. She knows that people and God are more important than time.
6. She lets the Holy Spirit activate her life.
7. She knows how to slow down and never be in a rush.
8. She fully believes that God already accepts her as who He created her to be.

Be Empowered

"But He knows the way that I take … I will come forth as gold," (Job 23:10).

So if there is any encouragement in Christ, any comfort from love, any participation in the Spirit, any affection and sympathy, complete my joy by being of the same mind, having the same love, being in full accord and of one mind. Do nothing from selfish ambition or conceit, but in humility count others more significant than yourselves. Let each of you look not only to his own interests, but also to the interests of others. Have this mind among yourselves, which is yours in Christ Jesus ...(Philippians 2:1–8, ESV)

"Humble yourselves before the Lord, and He will lift you up in honor," (James 4:10, NLT).

"In the same way, let your light shine before others, that they may see your good deeds and glorify your Father in heaven," (Matthew 5:16).

Thought to Ponder
To the Girl Who Has No Christian Home
By: Jordan Robinson

People say being a Christian is easy. They talk about how nice it is for them to go home to a loving Christian family. They tell me how easy it is to talk about their faith at home. I'm here to tell you my story about being the only Christian living in a non-Christian family. If you live in a non-Christian home, I want you to know you're not alone.

The hardest part about being in a non-Christian home is feeling alone and isolated from the rest of my family. I love my family, but they don't seem to care about and love my God the way I do. This makes me feel alone, distant, and almost abandoned. My emotions are everywhere, and sometimes it feels like I'm trying to walk through fast-moving rapids.

I get called names like "Bible Thumper" and "Jesus Freak." I get teased and asked a million questions about why I want to love my God. My family doesn't understand it when I turn on my Christian music, open up my Bible, or go to church. I try to get in a quick ten second prayer before my meals, just to escape more teasing. My family says they accept my faith, but they never seem to understand it.

It's quite a challenge to stay true to my faith. There are so many temptations and worldly things going on at home that it can be easy to forget to pray and read my Bible. I tell myself to stay strong and believe in myself. *I can do this*, I think *But living this way is the hardest thing I've ever had to do. It's hard to stand up for my faith when everyone around me is trying to tear it down.*

The best advice I can give you is to just be you! Don't worry about how other people see you, because God made you! You are created in His beautiful image. You are not alone.

When I'm teased at home, bullied, and feeling lonely, God helps me by giving me reassurance from His Word. I pull out my Bible and read Jeremiah 29:11–13:

"For I know the plans I have for you," says the Lord. "They are plans for good and not for disaster, to give you a future and a hope. In those days when you pray, I will listen. If you look for me wholeheartedly, you will find me." (NLT)

These words give me strength to overcome the name calling and the teasing. They give me strength to love them. I feel happy to know that when I'm alone, God is there right by my side every step of the way.

I'm a little seed who got planted in the ground, and with love, faith, and hope, I grew a little stronger day by day and bloomed into a beautiful flower. God has changed my life in so many ways by giving me strength and courage to get through each day. He has given me opportunities to do mission trips, be a counsellor at camp, and then go home to witness to my family. God has embraced me with open arms, and He has shown me how beautiful this world is. He has given me amazing friends that I call my family in Christ. I can talk about my faith and not be scared or ashamed. I can sing from my heart that I love God, because He has shown me not to be afraid. God has changed my life forever, and I can say that it has all been worth it.

Girls, I encourage you to keep your heads held high. Never let your family bring you down. Stay strong and put all your trust in God!

> *What is the price of two sparrows—one copper coin? But not a single sparrow can fall to the ground without your father knowing it. And the very hairs on your head are all numbered. So do not be afraid; you are more valuable to God than a whole flock of sparrows.* (Matthew 10:29–31, NLT)

Do not be afraid! God sees your pain. God sees your sleepless nights and every time your faith is challenged; it never goes unnoticed by our God. He is beside you through it all. Your life is a canvas, and God is the painter. Through your faith and trust in Him, God is slowly making you bloom into a beautiful flower so that no matter where you go—back to your non-Christian families, into your secular classroom, or out with your friends—you can live for Him.

chapter nine

What Are You Passionate About?

You can do anything you put your mind to. I believe in all of you. Never doubt yourself, even if everyone around you doubts you. Stand tall. Prove them all wrong. Each and every one of you have something amazingly special about you and don't let anyone tell you any different. Thank you for being you.[14]

CARRIE UNDERWOOD

I LOVE IT WHEN PEOPLE TELL ME I CAN'T DO SOMETHING, BECAUSE, honestly, that just makes me want to do it even more. In my last year of high school, I was told by a psychologist that I'd be setting myself up to fail if I ever attended university. I was diagnosed with a learning disability, attention deficient disorder, and a central auditory processing disorder when I was in the third grade. I had trouble focusing in class, comprehending material, and hearing full instructions. Since then, I've worked hard to develop learning strategies to cope with and adapt to my disability. God had given me the dream and passion to become a counsellor ever since I could remember, and the only way to do this was to attend a university. When the psychologist gave me this bad news, my mom took me to get ice cream. She said to me, "You are going to disregard everything that man just said to you, and you're going to trust God instead." In Matthew 19:26, Jesus says, "*With man this is impossible, but with God all things are possible.*"

Did you catch that? All things through Christ are possible! Sometimes it just takes dedication, determination, and a whole lot of prayer.

I want you all to know that in May of 2016, I graduated from Liberty University with a degree in psychology and counselling. I've loved every stage of my university career as I've grown as a critical thinker and learned fully that God can take what seems impossible and make it possible.

I also want you to know that university was not always an easy ride. Right after high school I went to Asbury University in Kentucky. I was excited to be in a place with such beauty and learn about psychology from a Christian perspective; however, I became very homesick— so homesick that I'd go two or three nights with no sleep. I lost almost ten pounds, and my grades were sliding. After only six and a half weeks, I was headed back home. I thought I'd thrown my whole future and career away, but God had different plans. You see, God sees the whole picture. In that moment, I thought I was failing, but God wasn't done with my story.

Passions and Desires

I believe God has given everyone passions, desires, and dreams that are waiting to burst from inside of us. Maybe the passions are just planted and still need to grow, but they're in there somewhere. Is there something that drives you to do courageous things? Is there a stirring in your heart to do something no one has thought of yet? Is there a passion deep in your soul that seems crazy and abnormal? Whatever it is, wake up, because most likely that passion is what God will use to bring people to Christ and help this crazy world.

Do you want to know my secret to living out my passions and dreams? My secret is to always remember that while living out my passions, I still place God as my identity. I have to remember to not forget about God as I chase after my dreams and goals. As I chase after Him, He unfolds the greatest road to my passion. Proverbs 16:3 says, "*Commit your actions to the Lord, and your plans will succeed,*" (NLT); "*Delight yourself in the Lord, and He will give you the desires of your heart,*" (Psalm 37:4, ESV).

As God unfolds the greatest road to my passion, He gives me new hopes and desires along the way. I started out with only one passion—to become a counsellor. Now I have the hope of teaching overseas. There's something about the unknown that excites me. So even though the doctors and some of my teachers and friends doubted my abilities, God didn't. It's all about being open to His leading and direction. It's like standing at the bottom of a mountain where there are many different paths to get to the other side. You can only take one step at a time, but God will show you the way.

Here are some questions to keep in mind as you let your passions grow. These come from Shannon Ethridge, who is a writer, speaker, and counsellor for women of all ages.

1. Is there a particular age group that I am drawn to? Children? Teens? Elderly?
2. Is there a particular group with special needs I feel a passion for?
3. Is there a particular issue at my school or in my community to which I am drawn?
4. What areas of ministry appeal to me the most?
5. What world problems create a hunger within me to become involved? World disasters? Poverty? The homeless?
6. What kind of difference do I want to make in the world?
7. What types of activities make me lose track of time?

8. What kind of activities can I not put down until I have completed them?[15]

Gifts, Talents, and Abilities

Living out your passion requires you to be aware of your gifts, talents, and abilities, as well as knowing how to apply them to your life. Your talents, gifts, and abilities came to you and only you for a reason and a purpose. If God gave it to you, He expects you to use it.

For example, for a while I hated going to my piano lessons. It was boring and I didn't want to make time for it. One day a friend said to me, "Sarah, you have such a gift for the piano. Keep honouring God by using your talent." That person gave me a new perspective on my piano lessons. I never thought of it as a talent God had given me. I started to play piano because God had given me the ability and gift for it. With this new perspective, I started to love piano. I'm grateful for my friend's kind words, as I'm still playing piano today.

I'm going to share with you a list of ideas of how to identify your gifts and talents. I pray and hope you'll be on your way to living out the passions and dreams God designed for you. Accept your gifts and abilities. Test them out and start using them for God's glory. Write out a list of what you love and enjoy doing by answering these questions:

1. What gives me the most joy?
2. What am I good at?
3. What are my goals? Write out a list of goals.
4. How do others view me? Get advice from others. Sometimes knowing how they view you can help you determine your gifts and abilities.
5. What is my favourite subject in school?
6. Is there a desire, dream, or goal inside of me that I still need to pursue?

Dream a God-Sized Dream

Never limit what God can do in your life. Is there something holding you back from your dreams and desires? Are you thinking that there's no way to conquer your dream because you aren't good enough? Instead of limiting yourself by what you cannot do on your own, remember that with God there are no limits. If God calls you to do it, then you can do it. He will give you the direction, guidance, and resources you need. He'll also show you that what seems impossible today, will be possible tomorrow.

You need to tap into your creativity. Creativity is the ability to imagine and believe possibilities for your life. You also need to be courageous. When you are courageous about your creativity, you start a fire of energy that will do nothing but build on your dreams and set your heart racing to fulfill your goals! Julia Cameron puts it perfectly:

> It is when we fire the arrow of desire, when we actually start a project, that we trigger the support of our dream. We are what sets things in motion; people and events resonate toward our fiery resolve. Energy attracts energy. We generate the energy and excitement, then others will give chase. Build it and they will come. Creative energy is energy. When we are worrying about creating instead of actually creating, we are wasting our creative mind. So, [once you] have [your] heart's desire, act on it. It is that action, that moving out on faith, that moves mountains.[16]

I also believe we need to surround ourselves with people who believe in our dreams and who can motivate us to keep going. I know I sure need this in my life! Surround yourself with the dreamers, the believers, and the thinkers. And make sure you have people in your life who believe in your greatness and calling, even when you don't see it yourself. Just remember to do the same for someone else too.

God can do anything—far more than you could ever imagine or guess or request in your wildest dreams! He does it not by pushing us around but by working within us, His Spirit deeply and gently within us (Ephesians 3:20, MSG).

God also instructs us to dream a God-sized dream by not letting our age limit us. Paul tells Timothy: "*Don't let anyone look down on you because you are young, but set an example for the believers in speech, in conduct, in love, in faith and in purity,*" (1 Timothy 4:12).

Seeking God's Calling

I think I have talked a lot about passions, talents, and gifts, but I want to zero in on one aspect that is critical for all of this—seeking out God's calling for your life. Sometimes our passions and dreams are tied to God's calling in our lives. Other times, we have to sacrifice our dream for something that God wants us to do. Sometimes this calling will be outside our comfort zone or beyond our wildest dreams, but when He calls, we must go, and until then, we must diligently seek Him out. We need to not just have a job, but seek to fulfill what God created us for!

I do, however, know without a doubt that each of us are already called to glorify God and live for Him in all aspects of our life. It is really that simple. Don't be afraid of His voice. Don't be fearful of the unknown. Instead, step out in boldness. Be brave. Stand firm.

He is preparing your heart and mind for His call. And what else I do know is that God never calls any of us to be unproductive, so get out from under your rock. Get out of your safety net. Live out your crazy, big dreams, but always be open and ready for God to pull you in deeper or in a different direction. You are smart and wise, so live like the woman who is seeking out God's call in every aspect of her life, so when the time comes to act, you will be like a roaring lion. And enjoy each step of that journey.

Integrity: Walk the Talk

Today, you can start making your dreams, passions, visions and calling a reality. Every single day counts. I want you to be the girl who turns her cant's into cans and her dreams into actual plans. Personal integrity is the key ingredient. It doesn't matter how big or small the goal is; integrity should always win. Integrity is the steadfast and constant endurance despite corruption. Integrity is about knowing our values, morals and standing firm in them. It is also about not allowing anything divide you. Integrity is being able to walk the talk. The simple daily actions are critical because they create the foundation. Every single day, we can make stepping stones by our actions that are aligned with our goals, dreams and even our calling. If we fail to make this action plan, we will fall off track and drift away.

Who are you when no one is watching? Do you take steps ahead, or are you living in past regret? Do you love to talk, but struggle with putting your words into action? Find time to take off the mask, be real with yourself and figure out what your true values and morals are. Then, stick to them. Be the girl who turns her doubt into hope, her fear into faith and her weaknesses into strengths.

You and I are created to make this life count. While a day to us may seem like no time to foster our dreams, God will use every day to shape your character for your specific calling. Isn't this amazing? Don't waste time. Don't back down. God desperately wants you to pay attention. He wants you to be fierce and real. Let's refuse to give our less when we could have the best in Christ. Every day is a gift. Only you can live it. Only you can take the action steps to get there. Do you want to live life to the fullest or do you want to settle for second best?

You also owe it to yourself to believe in your capabilities. If you believe, "I can't do it," guess what? You won't do it, but if you truly believe, "I can do it. I can conquer anything through Christ," then you are already making your first stepping stone in the right direction! I believe in you. And most importantly, God believes in you too. Stand up, girl. You can and will make these visions a reality. Start fostering your integrity and always remember to let God go before you. I am so excited for each and every one of you!

The Story of Queen Esther

Some of you are in the bondage of fear, but a head full of fear has no room for dreams. I want to share with you the story of Queen Esther and how she faced her fears and had great courage in the midst of a crisis. Esther was a Jewish orphan in a foreign land who became a queen. King Xerxes searched high and low for the perfect new queen. God chose Esther to be that queen; however, one of the king's servants despised the Jews and tricked the king into sentencing all the Jews to death. Esther had the biggest decision of her life to make—would she live out her calling to help free the Jews, or would she let fear, doubt, and unbelief cloud her mind? Esther was born for such a time as this.

> *Esther put on her royal robes and stood in the inner court of the palace, in front of the king's hall. The king was sitting on his royal throne in the hall, facing the entrance. When he saw Queen Esther standing in the court, he was pleased with her and held out to her the gold scepter that was in his hand. So Esther, approached and touched the tip of the scepter.*
>
> *Then the king asked, "What is it, Queen Esther? What is your request? Even up to half the kingdom, it will be given you."*
>
> *"If it pleases the king," replied Esther, "let the king, together with Haman, come today to a banquet I have prepared for him."*

"Bring Haman at once," the king said, "so that we may do what Esther asks."

So the king and Haman went to the banquet Esther had prepared. (Esther 5:1–5)

After attending a few of Esther's banquets, the king again asks Esther what she would like.

Then Queen Esther answered, "If I have found favor with you … and if it pleases you, grant me my life—this is my petition. And spare my people—this is my request. For I and my people have been sold to be destroyed killed and annihilated" …

King Xerxes asked Queen Esther, "Who is he? Where is he—the man who has dared to do such a thing?"

Esther said, "An adversary and enemy! This vile Haman!" (Esther 7:3–6)

Queen Esther's actions brought victory for the Jews, who overpowered their enemies. Esther became fearless. She completely trusted God and had faith to do what seemed impossible. With Him, we are all capable of this courage. Here are some tools to banish your fear:

• Trust in God.
• Do not do this alone. Have a good support system.
• Believe in yourself.
• Make the effort to work hard.
• Set goals.
• Be realistic.
• Always be ready to learn more.
• Never ever give up.

God did not create us to hide behind our fears, but to become fearless through Him. Becoming fearless doesn't mean you will never be afraid of anything, but that you will trust God with your future, living with the confidence and truth that you can conquer anything with Him by your side.

Sometimes God chooses the most unlikely women to fulfill His great purposes. God chose an ordinary orphan in a foreign land to free a host of people. God is calling you to fulfill His great purposes too. Will you start believing that your God-sized dream will come true? Will you cast out the fear from your mind and trust in God? You were born for such a time as this...

The Wisdom to Choose

Sometimes you'll pray and not "hear" a voice from God. You may also go for long periods of time not "feeling" God's presence. In these times, it's good to know how to properly discern what steps to take.

As we grow and mature, there can be hundreds of questions that fill our mind and pressure us to choose: What college do I choose? What will my major be? How do I go on the missions trip? Is he the right guy to date? How do I start up a ministry outreach program? How do I follow my passions and goals God's way if I don't hear His voice? God made us to be wise and sensible in how we make our decisions. He created us to know right from wrong and to glorify Him in everything. Whether it's a simple decision about whether to do house chores without complaining, or to say "yes" to a missions trip, you and I have the power to choose.

Some choices are scary, some hard, and some exciting. Here are some questions to ask yourself when making decisions:

1. Does it line up with God's truth? If you're reading God's Word daily and soaking it into your life, making wise choices will come easier. Make sure you're studying God's Word.

2. Are you praying about it? Sometimes we ask God for the answer but don't hear from Him right away, but praying about it shows that we trust God and still want to place Him first in our lives. You can never pray a prayer too many times. Continue to pray about the decision, even if you don't "hear" from God.

3. Is the timing of your decision right? Never make a rushed decision when you're tired, stressed, or anxious. God is never in a rush, so you shouldn't be either. Slow down when you make a decision.

4. Are you pleasing God or trying to impress others? When asked this question, the answer may become more clear. If you want to fulfill the task or duty for your own selfish ambitions, it may not be the best decision.

5. Do you have a good support system? God placed people in your life to help you make the tough decisions. While no one can make the final decision for you, asking advice from others can help guide you.

6. Does it seem way "over your head?" Don't be intimidated or overwhelmed in your decision making. Just because you think you're not equipped or smart enough to handle the challenge doesn't mean God doesn't want you to do it. God will provide everything you need and help guide you. Don't let anything hold you back.

7. Is it a desire deep in your soul? God knows the desires of your heart. If you have a passion and joy about a certain task, go do it!

8. Is it glorifying God? Remember, everything we do should be glorifying God in some way. If you're deciding between conforming to the world or conforming to God, always pick God's way.

Waiting Is Just Part of the Adventure

The goal of remaining faithful isn't that we do work for God, but that we allow Him to do His work *through* us. Now wait a minute … I want to be real before going further, because, honestly, this is so much easier to talk about than actually live out. It's completely valid to admit that faith can become stale, routine-like, and even lifeless. It's easy to fade and drift when we don't hear from God, and we can get lazy and stop looking to Him for guidance.

I think waiting is a test. Usually during a test the teacher silently anticipates how you'll do without his or her help. With God, we must remain hopeful and determined that His ways will prevail. An outcome and result will reign true!

I don't know if you've realized this yet, but His ways are not always what we first have in mind. His ways are not always what we want at that given moment; however, by remaining faithful through the waiting, His desires become ours and we step out into this amazing adventure. I also want you to appreciate the small moments. Place God over everything, and you'll start to see the still, divine moments that make living this crazy life so worth it!

We can want all we want, but God knows our deepest need. I know He has more in store for you than you can even imagine. Just hold on to Him … waiting is just part of the adventure. "*Rest in the LORD and wait patiently for Him; Do not fret because of him who prospers in his way,*" (Psalm 37:7. NASB).

Failure Is Never the End

When we fail at something, we start to believe we are a failure, but that's not truth. Failure is a part of this life, but it never has to have the last word. I have some news for you—failure is never final. Failure is always the opportunity to try again, begin again, and work harder.

I was a university dropout, but I still chased after God and my dreams. Once I got home from Asbury, I could have quit and left school, and my dreams, behind. Instead, I took it as a chance to try again and to do better. God wasn't finished with me, and today He is still inspiring me to be the best I can be. I can't wait to see what's ahead. I've decided that failure is not in my dictionary, and it shouldn't be in yours, either.

It takes a lot of hard work to conquer your goals and dreams. Yes, God is the God of impossibility, but we must do our part to work hard. Because of my learning disability, I spent many nights studying and reviewing what I'd learned in class instead of hanging out with my friends. I had to make flash cards, get tutored, and sit in the front row of my class. It took dedication, determination, and diligence. All I can say is that this hard work is paying off. You will find as you walk this journey that it won't always be fun and rosy. You'll have to make sacrifices and adapt to do your best. God honours hard work: "*A hard worker has plenty of food, but a person who chases fantasies has no sense,*" (Proverbs 12:11, NLT); "*Work brings profit, but mere talk leads to poverty,*" (Proverbs 14:23, NLT).

The next time you think you're failing at something, join me in allowing it to be an opportunity to try again. Will you give God the best you've got? I know that with God, you all will be champions. "*Humble yourselves, therefore, under God's mighty hand, that he may lift you up in due time,*" (1 Peter 5:6).

Here is my definition of success: be more like Christ today than you were yesterday, learning to sacrifice as Christ sacrifices, to serve as He serves, and to love as He loves.

The Whole World Is in His Hands

When I look at the night sky and see the work of your fingers—the moon and the stars you set in place—what are mere mortals that you should think about them, human beings that you should care for them? Yet you made them only a little lower than God and crowned them with glory and honor. (Psalm 9:3–5, NLT)

Have you ever looked up at the stars on a clear, dark night and thought about *what a mighty God we serve*? Have you ever looked at a waterfall and thought, *Wow, my God is creative*? Have you ever travelled by airplane and looked out the window to see the beautiful landscape below and realized that the whole world is in God's hands?

I remember being in Turkey a few years ago, following the journey of Paul through the book of Acts. God's Word came alive as I experienced the church of Corinth, the underground cities of Cappadocia, the ruins of Ephesus, and the land where my God stood. One of my favourite activities was soaring in a hot air balloon over Cappadocia. How glorious it was to see the earth from high up in the sky. I was able to see the glory of God shine from the sunrise, to the landscape, to the sky. I often wonder how anyone can't believe in my God?

God cares about every little detail. He makes butterflies from caterpillars, He thought of the evaporation of rain, and He even made you and me to show this world who the Creator truly is. Next time you look up at the night sky, appreciate the work of God's fingers. Appreciate everything He has given us, and know that your life is a part of His grand masterpiece.

Faith into Action

By faith, we understand that the entire world was formed by God's hands. It is by faith that we believe in our God and Saviour. Faith is the confidence and the hope for what will come to be. Faith gives us assurance about the things we cannot see. Let us put our faith in action, keeping our eyes on Jesus. There is joy awaiting us, for God has promised us so. Live in peace with everyone. Work hard to live out your passion, goals, and dreams God has given you. Be careful that you do not refuse to listen to the One who calls you to do it. Through it all, God says, "I will never fail you. I will never abandon you." The Lord is our helper. Who can stand against us? (Hebrews 11, 12 & 13)

Be Empowered

"For I can do everything through Christ, who gives me strength," (Philippians 4:13, NLT).

"Work willingly at whatever you do, as though you were working for the Lord rather than for people," (Colossians 3:23, NLT).

"The Lord says, 'I will guide you along the best pathway for your life. I will advise you and watch over you,'" (Psalm 32:8, NLT).

"God chose those despised by the world, things counted as nothing at all, and used them to bring to nothing what the world considers important," (1 Corinthians 1:28, NLT).

"I sought the Lord, and he answered me; he delivered me from all my fears," (Psalm 34:4).

"For God has not given us a spirit of fear and timidity, but of power, love, and self-discipline," (2 Timothy 1:7, NLT).

Thought to Ponder
TO THE GIRL WHO IS FEELING DEFEATED
BY: SARAH EVANGELINE

Last week I was feeling very defeated. I had no motivation to pray or read my Bible. It was like I was numb ... just so full of doubt. Does this sound familiar to any of you? Finally, late one night when I couldn't sleep, I opened my Bible to Ephesians 6, which told me:

> *Finally, be strong in the Lord and in his mighty power. Put on the full armor of God, so that you can take your stand against the devil's schemes ... Stand firm then, with the belt of truth buckled around your waist, with the breastplate of righteousness in place, and with your feet fitted with the readiness that comes from the gospel of peace. In addition to all this, take up the shield of faith, with which you can extinguish all the flaming arrows of the evil one. Take the helmet of salvation and the sword of the Spirit, which is the word of God. And pray in the Spirit on all occasions with all kinds of prayers and requests. With this in mind, be alert and always keep on praying for all the Lord's people.* (Ephesians 6:10, 14–18)

The morning after reading that scripture passage, my joy and strength were restored. The secret is that it really isn't my strength or my joy, but God's. His holy presence came alive in me again.

This defeat and fear you're facing is not from God; it's a feeling from the evil one. We should never base our faith or trust in God on a feeling. Feelings are fleeting and always changing. Just because you feel defeated and worn out today doesn't mean that God has left you or given up on you.

Knock that fear and doubt out by stepping out in faith. You see, faith is the exact opposite of fear. Faith helps us become fearless.

Being fearless doesn't mean you'll never feel fear; it simply means that you choose to rise above that feeling to let go and trust God instead. Faith is the confidence that God will do the impossible. Faith is the confidence that God will restore that joy and strength in you again.

Are you feeling defeated today? Is your mind full of doubt and fear? I challenge you to let God be your protector. Put on the full armour of God so that when troubles come your way, you will still be standing firm. Stay alert. And when that doubt creeps back into your mind, remember that God is still there.

I know today is going to be a good day. Why? Because I have decided to let God go before me, for He is my protector. I know that God holds this world in the palms of His hands, so whatever comes my way, He will be there to guide me through it. I also know that God is not finished with me yet. He is still writing my story. He is still writing yours too: *"But God's not finished. He's waiting around to be gracious to you. He's gathering strength to show mercy to you. God takes the time to do everything right—everything,"* (Isaiah 30:18, MSG).

Let the Author of life write your story today. No matter what comes your way, I hope you will be filled with His love and abundance of grace today. He is not finished with you yet.

chapter ten

Refuse to Conform to the Patterns of This World

We human beings don't realize how great God is. He has given us an extraordinary brain and a sensitive loving heart. He has blessed us with two lips to talk and express our feelings, two eyes which see a world of colours and beauty, two feet which walk on the road of life, two hands to work for us, and two ears to hear the words of love.[17]

MALALA YOUSAFZAI

PEOPLE ARE DRIVING THE LATEST AND FASTEST CARS. DO THEY KNOW where they are going? The sixteen-year-old girl dresses provocatively to be accepted by her boyfriend. Does she know where she's going? The group of friends get high off pot and cocaine. Do they know where they are going? The businessman cheats his way to the top, thinking no one will notice. Does he know where he's going? We see all the happy faces leaving the church building. Do they know where they are going?

Some days I feel so trapped by the culture and society's rules and regulations. Sometimes I feel so weighed down by the demands of people and the world that I forget I'm supposed to be living for God.

I've made my share of mistakes. I've said and done things I wish I could take back, but God changed me from the inside out. He restores my soul, and there is joy in the morning. When I look at the world, I wonder how people survive this life without knowing the King and Father of this world.

God loves the whole world, and He is everywhere. At twenty-three years of age, I've learned that I don't want to follow the patterns this world offers me. I want to look at the world and see it the way Christ sees it. Paul states:

> *Do not conform to the pattern of this world, but be transformed by the renewing of your mind. Then you will be able to test and approve what God's will is—his good, pleasing and perfect will.* (Romans 12:2)

The World Versus God

From the moment we're born, both God and the world have been grabbing for our attention. It's as if the world is on one shoulder and God is on the other. The world shouts our name, and God whispers it, so we must listen closely. We read in 1 Peter 2:9 that we are chosen. We are royal. We are God's very own possession. As a result, we can show others the goodness of God, for He called us out of darkness into His wonderful light.

People don't want to talk about the truth. We hide it under the rug and tell ourselves "it will be okay," or "it will never happen to me." We like to hide our mistakes to keep the "happy" and "perfect" smile. We see the hurting person, but we never dig deep enough to see what he or she is going through. We seek revenge when we should forgive. We let unrealistic expectations and pleasing other people rule our lives. We let labels, prescription bottles, and man's words define us. We justify and compromise our values and beliefs. We settle for worldly happiness when we could have pure joy. Could it be that our fast-consuming lifestyle is making us care so much about our own well-being and fame that we're missing out on God's purpose for us? "*Those who use the things of the world should not become attached to them. For this world as we know it will soon pass away*," (1 Corinthians 7:31, NLT).

I'm not suggesting that we have to be afraid of this world or hide ourselves from it. We need to be doing the exact opposite. I believe that if we protect ourselves from the world, we'll miss out on God's purpose for this life. We need to be out in the world. We need to know the dangers and see the brokenness. We need to take the risks. We need to know how to defend our faith and stand up for what we believe in. We have to stop being so self-centred and start to see the world the way God sees it.

We need to ask ourselves not what we can do for the world, but what does God want us to do for His world. In 1 John 5:4, we learn that "... *for everyone born of God overcomes the world. This is the victory that has overcome the world, even our faith*."

Someone once asked me, "Sarah, will you conquer the world, or will you let the world conquer you?" At twenty-three years of age, I know that my purpose for living this life is not just a "calling." I don't have to wait around for God to reveal a "sign" to me. My purpose and calling for this life is what Jesus already sent us all to do: invade the world for Christ and spread His glory and love everywhere we go. I'm not going to sit around waiting on God when He's the one waiting for me: "*As the Father has sent Me, I also send you*," (John 20:21). Christ has given us the amazing task to invade the world and proclaim His truth. Whether it's up the street to a neighbour or across the sea, it's the only way to find true fulfillment as we fulfill God's glorious purpose and plan for His world.

If you believe Jesus is the son of God and that He died for your sins, and you have asked Him for forgiveness and surrendered to His will, you have become a messenger of His truth. It's that simple. It's a shame that many Christians are missing out on the privilege of being God's light in the world because they misunderstand the purpose of being a follower of Christ.

Here is the truth: we are at war. Yes, this world has many amazing things, and God does hold the victory, but there is a war being waged between our human nature and our true identities as new creations in Christ. There may not be tanks or men running down our streets with guns, but it's a battle all the same. Do you feel it? Every human on this planet is tempted daily to say "yes" to the world and "no" to God. Even if 99 per cent of your being wants to please God in every way, that 1 per cent that doesn't submit to Him can take your whole body for granted and lead you down a road you thought you'd never go down.

I want to give you a brief, but clear, depiction of who Satan is and what he's trying to do to us. Satan is the thief and deceiver of this world. He loves it when we doubt God, and he rejoices when we fall into temptation. He tries to convince us that missions and living for Christ are optional. He likes to twist our minds into thinking it's okay to pick and choose what we want to do for Christ. Paul describes this well: "*Even Satan disguises himself as an angel of light. So it is no wonder that his servants also disguise themselves as servants of righteousness,*" (2 Corinthians 11:14–15).

The devil is real. Do not deny it. When we deny it, we let Satan have full reign over our hearts and minds. All Satan has to do is take your focus off of living for Christ. We must be familiar with the weapons we can use against the evil one. We must make prayer and solitude a priority, and construct our lives to stay self-disciplined in reading our Bibles and surrounding ourselves with fellow believers. We then have to apply what we learn to our life. We must take up our shield of faith.

We have to mentally, physically, and spiritually separate ourselves from the world's expectations and demands so that we can fully commit to God's ways and change the world instead of letting it change us. God didn't carry the bloody cross for us just so we could worship Him and keep our faith in a four-walls building. He wants us to live out our faith in this lost world so that others can know the truth and be saved. I have to remind myself that safety and security are not as important as knowing Christ and living according to His ways. In this life, you are not meant to sit on the sidelines. There are people in the world who are broken, beaten, and dying for something to fill their empty soul. This world is sick, and the only healer is Jesus. Christ has given you the power to save someone's life. You will get bruised, worn out, and exhausted, but your life will turn into an incredible legacy and journey. This is how the lost get found. This is how the empty can be filled. This is how God's purpose is fulfilled. Will you represent the world, or will you represent God to the world?

At twenty-three years of age, I have learned that I can't simply follow what everyone around me is doing. I need to question my motives, attitudes, and the reasons why I believe what I believe and why I do what I do. I'm finished settling for less than the fullness of life Christ gives me. I'm done trying to do everything on my own strength. I know that some days I may not hear His voice, but I will remember the promise and purpose He designed for me long ago.

At the end of the day, I don't want to represent my work, university, or even my church. I want to represent Christ—not because it's my duty as a believer, but because it's a privilege to know I'm living for God and have His purpose and meaning for living. He is my greatest adventure, and I want to invade the world for Him. I refuse to conform to the patterns of this world. How about you?

Remember that the world shouts your name, but God whispers it. We must listen closely. The world says, "Do more! Be Busy! Do what you want to do when you want to do it!" God says, "*Be still and know that I am God*," (Psalm 46:10).

God will be exalted above the earth. God will be exalted above this world. Jesus said, "*In this world you will have trouble. But take heart! I have overcome the world*," (John 16:33).

How to Live Among Unbelievers

When was the last time you spoke to an unbeliever? As I said earlier, refusing to conform to this world doesn't mean we hide from it; it means we go out and proclaim God's name to the world. Therefore, in this crazy world, it is critical that you and I know how to live among unbelievers.

There was a time in my life when all my friends were Christian. I went to a Christian school, I had a Christian family, and I went to church every Sunday. I was safe and protected from the world's corrupt ways; however, when I finally got my first job in a secular workplace, I met and gained some friends who were unbelievers. It was hard at first, but I remembered that all I needed to be was real and myself.

I started to have coffee with a girl who had moved from Florida all the way to Chatham, Ontario. I was up front with her and told her that I was a Christian. I thought she was so brave to leave her family and start a new life here in my city. We had a lot in common. We had travelled to many of the same places, and we loved watching movies together and eating brownies. She had lots of questions about my faith, and I answered them and listened to her stories. I learned that being friends with unbelievers is a part of what God created us to do. So when was the last time you spoke to an unbeliever?

The key to living among unbelievers is to know how to influence them for Christ without letting them influence you in a bad way. Another key is to make sure you have a good Christian support system in place that can support you as you witness: "*Keep away from worldly desires that wage war against your very souls. Be careful to live properly among your unbelieving neighbors,"* (1 Peter 2:12, NLT).

I encourage you to make friends with unbelievers. Set up strong boundaries to make sure you influence them and not the other way around. Be careful and be aware of the dangers, but get out and proclaim God's name to the world.

The Myth of Safety

Safety is not always an option when we choose God over the patterns of this world. Instead, we must take risks, and a lot of them. A risk occurs when we step into the unknown, unsure of what may happen. A risk allows loss and injury to take place for the sake of the cross. Someone once said to me, "Faithfulness and trust are mine, but the results are God's."

Risks are woven into our being the moment we accept Christ as our Lord and Saviour. You actually took a risk back in chapter one when I asked you to step into the unknown. We'll never be able to avoid risks, no matter how hard we try. John Piper in his book, *Don't Waste Your Life*, gives insight into the myth of safety:

> All of our plans for tomorrow's activities can be shattered by a thousand unknowns whether we stay at home under the covers or ride the freeways. One of my aims is to explode the myth of safety and to somehow deliver you from the enchantment of security. Safety doesn't exist. Every direction you turn there are unknowns and things beyond your control.[18]

See the World Through God's Eyes

I'm going to summarize the story of creation for you, but I encourage you to open your Bibles and read it from Genesis 1. In the beginning,

God created the heavens and the earth. On the first day, God broke through the darkness and gave us light. On the second day, God created the waters and the sky. On the third day, God made land and vegetation possible. Next, He gave us night and day. On the fifth day, God created great sea creatures and every living thing. On the sixth day, God said, "*Let us make human beings in our image, to be like us. They will reign over the fish in the sea, the birds in the sky, the livestock, all the wild animals on the earth,*" (Genesis 1:26, NLT). So God created human beings in His own image. On the seventh day, God looked out on all He had created and said, "It is good."

It all happened because it's not about you. It all happened because it's not about me. It's about our God, our brilliant Creator. God looked out on His creation and said it was very good. The word "good" means moral, virtuous, worthy, blameless, wholesome, beneficial, reliable, advantageous, useful, and trustworthy. So why are we here? Why do we have to live in this crazy world? How can we truly see this world the way God sees it? Rick Warren says there are three ways God views life: life is a test, life is a trust, and life is a temporary assignment.

First, we can see the world through God's eyes when we endure the test. Even if we can't feel God's presence, we can still honour and obey Him. Enduring the test means watching how we react to situations; it means choosing God over a lustful thought, and spending quality time with Him every day. It means remaining faithful to God.

Secondly, we can see the world through God's eyes when we understand that this life is about a trust. Are we going to use our time, money, and energy to make the most of every opportunity? Can God trust us with the little things so that He can give us the big things?

Lastly, we see the world through God's eyes by knowing and understanding this world is only temporary. God asks us to stop flirting with the world and live as if heaven is our home, not this world!

I will do the most I can for Christ while I'm still here, but I am fixing my eyes on heaven: "*So we fix our eyes not on what is seen, but on what is unseen, since what is seen is temporary, but what is unseen is eternal,*" (2 Corinthians 4:18). Now it's my turn to ask you the question: Will you conquer the world, or will you let the world conquer you?

A Call to Holy Living

Think clearly and exercise self-control. Live as obedient children to God. Do not slip back into your old ways of living to satisfy your own desires. Now, you must be holy in everything you do, just as God chose you to be holy. And remember that the heavenly Father will judge and reward you according to how you live. It was the precious blood of Christ that bought you for a chance to live higher than the ways of this world. God chose you, long before this world began. Through Christ, you have come to trust in Him. So place your hope and faith in Him. Be sincere in how you love each other. Your new life will last forever because it comes from the eternal, living word of God. People are like grass; their beauty is like a flower in the field. The grass withers and the flower fades, but the truth of God will live forever. (1 Peter 1:13–25, paraphrased)

Be Empowered

"Let the spirit renew your thoughts and attitudes. Put on your new nature, created to be like God—truly righteous and holy," (Ephesians 4:23–24, NLT).

"Do not love the world or anything in the world. If anyone loves the world, love for the Father is not in them," (1 John 2:15).

"No eye has seen, no ear has heard, and no mind has imagined what God has prepared for those who love Him," (1 Corinthians 2:9, NLT).

"I am leaving you with a gift—peace of mind and heart. And the peace I give is a gift the world cannot give," (John 14:27, NLT).

Thought to Ponder
To the Girl Who Is Too Busy
By: Rebekah McNeilly

I wish I could say I've thought long and hard about what to share with you beautiful ladies, but I didn't. Life is very busy sometimes (always), and the most important things tend to get pushed far down on the list. So here I am, in the passenger seat on the way to Kingston, driving through a downpour of rain, and writing without an established train of thought.

This is how we do life. We have a smattering of thoughts and big dreams, hopes, excitements, and Instagram-worthy picture ideas, but it often feels as if so few of them pan out.

Here's the thought: How much does the pursuit of self-betterment take away from the pursuit of God's glory and ultimately the pursuit of souls? Here's my ugly truth: I run because I want to be thin and pretty. I shop (a lot) because I want to wear the cutest and trendiest outfits. I work hard in school because I want to be a success story, and I want to do it at a young age, and I want people to notice.

You're likely not in as bad shape as I, but I'm confidant we all have similar desires— desires to do well, which Ecclesiastes even tells us we should desire. It's certainly not wrong to want to do well, but at some point in time ... at least in my own life ... doing well for God became doing well for me. It's quite possible that's always how it's been.

At various times Jesus called on His disciples to take up their crosses and follow Him. He also told them to leave everything they owned to follow Him. He explained that anything that replaces Him is an idol. We should hold on to no earthly thing. Jesus explained that it's very hard for a rich man to get into heaven. The Old Testament says beauty is fleeting (Proverbs 31:30). The message is simple, concise, and frankly aggressive: give up everything the world says is important and just love God.

I think I may be an apathetic, self-absorbed Christian. Well, folks, this was not my plan. In fact, among my little-girl dreams were wild adventures in Africa running around in sackcloth with elephants and orphan children. Slowly as I got older, and the world got bigger, and the many voices telling me what matters got louder, the sackcloth and orphan children were forgotten. Now I desire to serve God—just as long as I also have enough money to buy a house. I want to be in ministry, but only in Toronto, because that's where my whole life is. Oh, and a sackcloth? Sorry, that's not how I roll.

Perhaps what I'm about to write is overly aggressive, and I'm confidant there are those who do not share my opinion, but I truly believe that we can't have both. We can't love ourselves, our money, and our pretty lives while at the same time truly, painfully, and rightfully love our God. I don't know what that actually means, tangibly, because I know very wealthy people who love God. I also know some very pretty people who serve God selflessly. What I do know is that for all of us, the righteous and unrighteous alike, those who serve and those who lounge, until none of those things matter to us, the plight of our Lord doesn't either. So what do we do?

This leads me to the simplest, most repeated, most neglected solution to our idol-anxiety-filled-human ways: we must spend time with Yeshua, Abba, Jesus. Oswald Chambers said, "We can remain powerless forever … by trying to do God's work without concentrating on His power, and by following instead the ideas that we draw from our own nature."[19] This is truth. I can't give up all of my idols and then present myself to my God as an empty canvas. My humanness simply doesn't allow for it. I can't wake up tomorrow and stop desperately clinging to my parents; I am not strong enough.

I have a final example of what this means to me. I started dating someone during my second year of university. It quickly became the most serious relationship I've ever had. During my first two years at school, I experienced that sick anxiety over missing my parents, worrying they were going to be taken from me, and desperately needing to be at home every second I was away. When I started dating, this remained true during the first months. Slowly, as I spent more time with him, I grew to know him and love him. I became increasingly comfortable with him. I also felt good about myself as I spent time with this steady, loving, and encouraging man of God. The craziest thing happened: I stopped needing to go home as desperately. If we were to spend time getting to know God through and through, allow ourselves to be entirely vulnerable with Him, and even get excited about the love story that would (inevitably) develop, it would change our lives. Would it rid us of our anxiety? Would it cause us to care less and less about the material things of this world? Would it give us such an abundance of love that we couldn't help but love others?

I have something even better than ten steps for you. I have one step—seek God. Every morning, every night, at lunch time, before class, before you talk to your best friend, after you make a wrong choice. Get to know Him. Learn to desire Him. Watch what He does.

chapter eleven

Love, Boys,
and God

*I think there's a real delicate balance that God calls
us to when we are single. I don't think He calls
us to put our dreams on the shelf to the level that
we're just dead to it, because then we're not being
true or honest. I think God calls us to come in our
vulnerability as singles and say "Lord, I long
for this, I really desire to be married,
but I trust you with this dream.*[20]
REBECCA ST. JAMES

WHEN I WAS SIXTEEN YEARS OLD, I HAD MY FIRST BOYFRIEND. I WAS SO excited, I was so "in love," and I didn't know at all what I was doing! After only three months, the relationship ended. I was heartbroken, and I felt like my world was falling apart. Over a boy? Yes. That seems so crazy to me now, but back then I used to place boys ahead of God. After my first break-up, I didn't date for another three years, because I had to work on my relationship with God first and love myself second. You see, I didn't know that my identity was in Christ, so I put all my worth and identity in that boy. When the relationship ended, I should have been able to fall back onto God, not my own two feet.

Boys are everywhere. Dating is pushed on us at a very young age. Sex appeal is on every cover magazine and television show. We live in a crazy world that has love mixed up and used for all the wrong reasons. I want to share with you how to experience love, dating, and boys the way God intended us to.

God's Love for You and Me

Love is mentioned over 281 times in the Bible. I believe God is the Author and Giver of love, so we should all be looking to Him for the answers when it comes to love. The Bible shows us four types of love. The first one is agape love, which is represented by God's love towards us: "*For God so loved the world that He gave His only and begotten Son, that whosoever believeth in Him should not perish, but have everlasting life,*" (John 3:16, KJV). Paul describes this type of love in detail:

> *Love is patient, love is kind. It does not envy, it does not boast, it is not proud. It does not dishonor others, it is not self-seeking, it is not easily angered, it keeps no record of wrongs. Love does not delight in evil but rejoices with the truth. It always protects, always trusts, always hopes, always perseveres. Love never fails.*
> (1 Corinthians 13:4–8)

The second kind of love is phileo, which means to have an interest in someone like a friend. Storge is affectionate love for a family member.

The last type of love is eros, which refers to desire and longing for romantic love. God gave this kind of love for men and women to share in marriage. Such love is illustrated in the Song of Solomon.

The golden rule while living this life is to love the way God loves us. This is the highest form of love:

You shall love the Lord your God with all your heart and with all your soul and with all your strength and with all your mind, and your neighbor as yourself. (Luke 10:27, ESV)

Dear Future Husband

Do you love God?

Can you love someone more than yourself?

Do you love yourself?

Can you embrace all of the qualities God gave you?

Can you love someone else the way God loves you?

I ask you these questions because I'm a true believer that we should love God first before we start dating. The closer we are to Jesus, the easier it will be to see which relationships are blessings and which ones are dangerous. I also believe we should know how to love others and how to accept ourselves before dating. I know you and I will never be perfect, but when we truly know that we love God first and accept ourselves, love and boys will make more sense. I'm not married yet, but I'm going to share with you what I have learned through my relationship with God, through my previous boyfriends, my two brothers, and through my male friendships.

First of all, you need the power to pray for your future husband. He's out there somewhere, facing all the impossibilities you are. He needs your support and prayers starting today. Every day I try to make a point to pray for my future husband. It gives me shivers and excitement to know that God knows where he is. Praying for him not only helps him in that moment, but it helps prepare our hearts for when we meet.

God designed Christians to be married to other Christians. Paul talks about this in his second letter to the Corinthians: "*Do not be yoked together with unbelievers. For what do righteousness and wickedness have in common? Or what fellowship can light have with*

149

darkness?" (2 Corinthians 6:14). How can we be with someone who doesn't have the light of Christ in them as we do? How can the dark and light work together if they are constantly in battle? We should also think wisely about marrying someone who doesn't follow and chase after God. Here is what can happen if you are unequally yoked:

1. It may stunt your growth with Christ. Just think … if you're dating someone who doesn't believe in God, he may influence you in a negative way and steer you off the path of your relationship with God.

2. It may burden you if you think you have to carry your faith for two people. Instead of him encouraging you in your relationship with God, you may be blinded to think you have to carry out you own faith for the both of you.

3. You may start to lose your own faith. If you're constantly around someone who doesn't believe in your God, you may be influenced negatively.

4. God may lose His place of priority in your heart. God must be first in any relationship. How can God be first if the boy doesn't even know God?

5. You may start to believe that you can win him over by dating him. Never, ever date a guy just to see if you can win his heart for the Lord. This can be so dangerous.

6. You may feel the need to change your values and morals.

You are chosen and loved by the One true God. He doesn't want you to settle for anything less than you deserve. I'm not going to tell you that being equally yoked with a true believer is going to be an easy life. People are people, but God knew what He was doing by encouraging us to be bonded only with a true believer. If we want to live a life chasing after God, how can we become one with a person who doesn't follow

God as well? There are a lot of boys out there who call themselves Christian, yet they live a totally different lifestyle. Save yourself for someone who loves God more than you, who values your worth in Christ, and who does everything he can to encourage you to walk with the Lord. Every guy will have imperfections, just like you, but he needs to have Christ in his life in order for any relationship to work.

Be friends first. I've learned that the best way to enter into a romantic relationship is to have a good foundation in friendship. I know this because I dated two Christian men who were great boyfriends, but we didn't actually become good friends. I found it hard to be myself. I've also dated one of my best friends. He and I were good friends for almost two years before we started dating. The relationship didn't last, but because we had a foundation of friendship, he's still a good friend to me today.

I also want to caution you about the three words "I love you." They are sacred. They are special. Those are three words that can change your life, but I don't want you to give away your love too quickly. It's a big deal to say "I love you" to a guy. Just know that your love is sacred, so value and cherish it. Save it. I also want to encourage you to let yourself fall in love. I have fallen in love and I know it is beautiful, wonderful, and the best thing I have done. Stay true to your values and cherish your love, but when you meet the right guy, don't be afraid of love. You are worthy of love.

When a relationship doesn't work out, remember that God is still in control. I remember dating a guy and thinking he was the "one" I wanted to spend my entire life with; however, we broke up a few weeks later. I wasn't as devastated as I was during my first breakup, because I knew it was all in God's power. When you truly care about and love a person, you should wish them the best. You're allowed to be hurt, and you're allowed to be sad, but you're not allowed to seek revenge. Be mature and honour God in the way the relationship ends.

Let go. I mean that literally. Let go. As women, we're always thinking about and looking for our husbands. It's easy to want to chase after every guy because he might be the "one." It's also easy to overthink everything and worry about "what if." Relax. God has it covered. We shouldn't just sit at home, waiting for him to ring the doorbell and propose, but we can be assured that God is working it all out. Let go and trust God with the bigger picture.

Marriage is the second most important decision we'll make in life. After choosing to accept God as your Lord and Saviour, who we choose to marry impacts our life in a major way. I'm not saying this to make you scared, but to make you excited for what is ahead. Even though I'm not married, I can't wait for the day I meet my husband.

A word of caution—even though I'm encouraging you to wait for that guy who chases after God with all his heart, don't expect him to be perfect. I encourage you to read over my list and then make up your own ten characteristics you want in your future husband. This is a two-fold rule—don't settle for less than you deserve, but also allow grace for imperfections. I once heard Gary Thompson, a motivational speaker who teaches about marriage from a godly perspective, say that there are six important aspects when it comes to choosing our husband. I've adapted those into my list that I want to share with you:

1. A man who is an active follower of Christ. This means that the Holy Spirit is active in his life.

2. A man who tries his best to react to situations with love and grace. Does he avoid conflict? Does he react with violence? Does he manipulate or control the situation? I want a man who knows how to handle conflict.

3. A man who respects his own family and friends and can respect my family and friends. The way he treats his own family is the way he will ultimately treat me.

4. A man who prays. I want Him to be seeking God when he is alone and when he is in public.
5. A man who is a hard worker and a good leader.
6. A man who shows true humility. He serves not to impress people, but because he is passionate about serving God.
7. A man who would make a good father. He's not only going to be my husband, but also the father of my children.
8. A man who is my best friend and knows how to work on a team.
9. A man who believes I'm still pretty without any makeup on.
10. A man who knows how to encourage me in my own walk with God.

As you write your own list, make sure that whatever you add to it also applies to your own life. For instance, I can't expect those wonderful ten characteristics from my future husband if I'm not willing to strive for them as well. If I want my man to be an active follower of God, I must be following God. If I want my man to respect my family and friends, I need to know how to respect him and his family. While I remain hopeful, knowing God is crafting my future husband as I write these words, I know I will love him through his imperfections. As you write your list, start putting that list into practice in your own life.

So many young people are trapped in the thinking that they have to wait until they meet "the one." While I believe that God designs and crafts people to be together, I know my future husband won't necessarily be "the one," but will be someone I choose to be committed to for the rest of my life. He will make my dreams come true, and I will fall in love with him, but those feelings may fade with time, because feelings are fleeting, but commitment is grounded. I know I won't wake up every morning deeply in love with the man beside me.

That is because we are both imperfect, and only God completes us. However, when I marry, I will decide every morning that I will love him because we have chosen to be partners for life. Don't be caught up in the love stories of movies … they aren't real. Commitment, trust, and loyalty are what is real. So instead of searching high and low for "the one," wait for someone who understands that marriage and love are more a commitment than a feeling.

The True Meaning of Purity

When I think of the word purity, I see a girl who loves the Lord over all other men and lusts of this world. She calls Christ her first love and King of her heart and mind. She doesn't let boys or her own vanity get in the way of her relationship with God. She's not perfect, but she finds her self-worth in Christ alone. Jesus fills her cup, and everything afterwards is just an overflow of that grace. She is dressed in white and standing before the cross.

Part of remaining pure is loving God first, before any man or lusts of this world. I encourage you to be the girl who goes after her dreams and passions and doesn't let a boy damage them. Be the girl who still loves God first, even when you have the boyfriend. Remember, you don't change who you are for anyone or anything.

Purity isn't just about resisting sexual temptation; purity affects all areas of one's life. It impacts what we watch, how we dress, and who we surround ourselves with—literally everything. Most people refer to purity as "staying pure until marriage." I agree, but I believe purity is a life-long goal. This means resisting all temptations and lusts of this world to choose God instead. As for me, I still want to seek a life of purity even after I walk down the aisle and marry my husband. It brings me abundant joy to honour and live for God in this way. I hope it brings some encouragement and joy into your life today.

We've talked about how our bodies are holy temples. Now I want to give you the longer version of that scripture passage.

> *Run from sexual sin! No other sin so clearly affects the body as this one does. For sexual immorality is a sin against your own body. Don't you realize that your body is a temple of the Holy Spirit …? You do not belong to yourself, for God bought you with a high price. So honor God with your body.* (1 Corinthians 6:18–20, NLT)

> *When you follow the desires of your sinful nature, the results are very clear: sexual immorality, impurity, lustful pleasures, idolatry, sorcery, hostility, quarrelling, jealousy, outburst or anger…drunkenness, wild parties, and other sins like these. Let me tell you again, as I have before, that anyone living that sort of life will not inherit the Kingdom of God. But the Holy Spirit produces this kind of fruit: love, joy, peace, patience, kindness, goodness, faithfulness, gentleness, and self-control.* (Galatians 5:19–23, NLT)

Throughout the Bible, God calls us to a life of purity: "… *be holy because I am holy,*" (Leviticus 11:45, NLT); "*Be an example to all believers … in the way you live, in your love, your faith, and your purity,*" (1 Timothy 4:12, NLT); "*Abstain from every form of evil,*" (1 Thessalonians 5:22, ESV).

We must honour God and our future husbands with our bodies. This world tells us that sex is a normal part of everyday life. Sex is something God created to be beautiful, fun, and holy within the sanctity of marriage. There's much controversy on this subject, and many may disagree with me, but I believe God intended all sexual activity for marriage. When sex becomes a normal part of our everyday life, we're not only hurting God, but our future marriage.

I know there are temptations. I know you may have made past mistakes. Trust me, I've been there, but you don't have to live that way any longer. This is where grace comes in. You can ask God for forgiveness and ask Him to help you live a better lifestyle. Today, you can have a second chance. I will talk more about this in just a minute.

It's hard to know how to get rid of our sinful nature. Remember, purity is a life-long goal that we all need to be striving for. I've composed a list of tools to help you remember how to do this:

1. Be wise in your decisions. Recognize the temptation and sin before it gets too big for you to handle. In 1 Corinthians 6:18, Paul says, "*Run from sexual sin! No other sin so clearly affects the body as this one does,*" (NLT).

2. Stay in the light. If you're doing something with your boyfriend that doesn't feel right, it probably isn't: "*But if you fail to do this, you will be sinning against the Lord; and you may be sure that your sin will found you out,*" (Numbers 32:23).

3. Be able to discern sin's many disguises.

4. Don't hang out with the wrong people. Have a good support system.

5. Set boundaries: "*People with integrity walk safely, but those who follow rooked paths will be exposed,*" (Proverbs 10:9, NLT).

6. Don't let yourself get worn down.

7. Don't believe everyone is doing it. Don't just do it because you think others are and it's okay.

8. Know that God sees everything: "*The Lord still rules from heaven. He watches everyone closely, examining every person on earth,*" (Psalm 11:4, NLT)

9. Remember and believe that God is there to help you every step of the way.

To the Girl Who Doesn't Feel "Pure" Anymore

I have been in a place in my life where I didn't think I was pure anymore. I've dated the good guys and the bad guys. I've been in an emotionally abusive relationship, and I've been with someone who thought he could own my body. My emotionally abusive boyfriend thought he could twist the Bible and manipulate me to love him, because he believed God said we were meant to be together. Since I was only sixteen at the time, I believed him and thought I loved this "man of God." After a few months of the constant manipulation of my thoughts, he became obsessed with me. Instead of feeling safe and secure, I felt stuck and unable to move and get away from someone I thought I'd have to spend the rest of my life with. I was so young and vulnerable, I didn't truly understand that not every Christian guy out there follows after God's heart. Finally, after my parents and advisors got involved, I was able to break free. I never saw that man again.

A few years later, I was in another relationship that I thought would be wonderful. He was a solid, Christian guy (from the outside looking in), and he came from a good family. It didn't take long, however, before he thought he could have full reign over my body in a sexual way. The worst part is that I let him. While I was still a "virgin," I was left feeling powerless, weak, and defenseless. I remember feeling disgusting, broken, and so far from God. *How did I end up in this position again*? I vowed and promised myself to be so careful. This time, I knew how to say goodbye and move forward, but it took a long time for me to heal. For months I had nightmares, and many times I thought I'd never be worthy of being whole again. I felt like I'd cheated on my future husband, and that guilt followed me around. I am sad to admit that I even walked away from God for half a year before I realized I could be made holy again. It was a long journey, but the truth is God never left me; it was only because of my shame, guilt, and regret that I felt separated from Him.

To the girl who is feeling broken, lost, empty, disgusting, and worthlessness, and who thinks she'll never be able to be called God's daughter again, I want to give you hope. Do not lose faith. God redeemed me from this place of brokenness many years ago, and He can and will do the same for you. God has never left your side. He's not finished with your story. He sees your heart and longs for you to cry out to Him. Remember, guilt and shame don't come from God. His gifts are only love, grace, and a warm embrace. Remember also that marriage is something to dream about and look forward to. Until then, we must rebuild that relationship with God. I know I am whole and pure because Christ has washed me and made me whole. He will do the same for you. I cannot wait to look my husband in the eye as I walk down the aisle knowing I waited for him—only him. It will be the best walk I ever take. I know it.

Allow God to Write Your Love Story

Something beautiful happens when God writes our love story. We know His ways are better, we know that His ways are true, and we know that He is perfect. I believe God is the Author of romance. So why not give God the pen to write our love story too?

I used to have my whole life planned out. I was going to graduate from university by the age of twenty-two, I'd be married by age twenty-six, and I'd start having my children by age twenty-nine. You may already have your wedding dress and colours all picked out. Today, I'm asking you to slow down and take a look inside your heart. When we allow God to write our love story, amazing things start to happen:

1. You can love your husband even before you meet him. God knows exactly where your husband is and what he is doing. God knows when you will meet.

2. You start to have eyes only for your future husband. Instead of

being distracted by every guy that looks your way, you remain prayerful and hopeful, knowing it's all in God's timing.

3. You can start practicing purity for your marriage. We talked about purity already. Start putting what you have learned into action.

4. You will start to understand that love is much more than just a feeling. Love is a commitment. Love is a promise. Love is loyal.

5. You can work on your relationship with God. I mean, even when we're dating and married we should never stop growing with God, but this is an opportunity for you to stop trying to take control of you love life, and give it up for God to handle.

6. Write letters to your future husband. I know one girl who wrote many love letters to her husband. She gave him all of her letters on their wedding night. Even when she was lonely and doubted God, she wrote to him.

7. You can protect your virginity. Allowing God to write your love story can help you protect your body for your future husband. You're already "taken," but you're in the waiting period.

The Purpose of Being Single

There is purpose in being single. Yes, it can be a struggle, but you're single for a reason. I know a girl who was single until she was thirty-five. She never dated, because she knew God wanted her to wait for that special person He'd planned out for her. While she was single, she served God in the best way she could. She was a well-known teacher in her town, and she led a Bible study every week. People would ask her, "Don't you ever want to go out and start dating? Aren't you worried you will never get married?" She would simply reply, "No, because I know my God has that covered."

One day, when she was thirty-five, a young man started attending her Bible study. Over the course of two years they became very good friends. One night, this young man (who was also in his thirties) rang her doorbell to ask her a question: Will you marry me? Today, they are happily married with four beautiful children. I'm not saying we are all meant to be single until age thirty-five, but while you are single, find the grace and peace my friend did.

I told you this story because it's vitally important that you are content being single before you start dating. It doesn't mean that you'll have all the answers, but it does mean that you'll already be confident in who Christ made you to be. Remember, you want to date someone for the right reasons, not to fill you own insecurities. After I dated my second boyfriend, I realized that I was dating him to fill my own insecurities, and that I was chasing after this boy more than God. When the relationship ended, I promised God that I would be single for a whole year. During that year, I grew with God more than at any other time, and I wouldn't change that for the world. So remember … there is a strong purpose in being single.

Let's Talk Boys

You may be asking yourself a number of questions: What if there are no guys left out there who love God? What if there are no guys left who want the same kind of purity I want? These questions run rapidly through a lot of women's minds. I was able to ask some men for their perspectives on women, purity, love, and God. These are real guys with real answers. Here were some of the questions and their comments:

What kind of woman do you want?
- I want a woman who has mystery—a girl who guards her heart.
- I want a woman who is different from the culture's standards.
- I want a woman who is focused on God and who doesn't get distracted by me.

•I want a woman who doesn't need to throw herself at me, but allows me to win her heart.

One guy said this about a godly woman:

A godly woman is a girl who knows that she's not perfect, but she embraces who she is as being unique and made in the image of God. She loves others as themselves and puts an emphasis on prayer and God's Word in her own life and the lives of those around her.

Another boy defined a godly woman as "a girl who worships God and lives for Him; she respects her body, prays, and follows God's Word."

A man defined purity this way:

I believe purity is a state of being rather than never having committed sexual sin. A lot of people think purity is waiting till marriage before having sex. While sex is meant to be enjoyed inside marriage, what if we don't wait and commit that sin? Have we lost that purity? The Bible says that Jesus took the sin of the world upon himself to cleanse people of their sin. It's almost as if purity is a white robe. Sometimes we make bad decisions and get into the mud. We become dirty, and we even feel dirty. But Jesus comes and takes off our dirty clothes, cleanses us, and gives us a clean white robe, as if we hadn't been dirty before. Purity is about trusting in Jesus, the one who is truly pure and makes us more like Him.

Another guy defined purity this way:

Purity means striving to be holy in thought, word, and action. Everyone stumbles and makes mistakes, but it's important to confess and move forward with the hope and intention of not allowing the slip-ups to keep occurring, or else sin will rule in our lives.

When asked to talk about love, one said:

In order to love her, a guy has to have some recognition or understanding of who she is. A man cannot know what she feels, so he has to ask her how she feels. You can never force love. The best advice I can give a girl is for her to be herself.

Another guy said this about modesty and beauty:

God made men to be visually stimulated; we can't help but notice when girls expose their bodies. However, if a guy is interested in a girl for a long-term relationship or to be his wife, he's looking for a girl who is attractive by not showing off "too much."

I asked a guy what attracts him to girls, and he said, "A girl who is joy-filled. A girl who doesn't gossip or laugh about others, but goes through life with a joy that comes from God."

Someone else added to the discussion of beauty by saying:

A girl's outward appearance will change with time, but her personality and character will be with her for her whole life. Therefore … and I think I can say this for a lot of guys … we want her beauty to lie in her personality and character. I want a girl who cares more about her heart than what she's wearing.

One of the men was very wise and gave a note of caution to women everywhere:

I hate the many lies society throws at women. All women are beautiful and need to push away those lies from Satan. Men, including myself, need to actively fight off these lies by reminding our sisters-in-Christ of their absolute worth and beauty.

Finally, I asked the group of guys if there was anything they wanted to tell their future wives. One wrote this beautiful letter:

I have visions of being with a loving and godly woman one day. I truly believe part of my calling in life is to serve my future wife in such a deep way. I would want her to know that my ultimate desire in our marriage is to make her happy and help her to grow closer to Jesus. I also want my future wife to know that I'm praying for her and trusting that God will prepare me to be a godly man for her. I'm far from perfect, but I desire our future marriage to be defined by purity, integrity, and a full dependence on God's direction and leading.

Another man wrote this for his future wife:

I'm excited to spend the rest of my life with you some day. I'm not perfect. I make a lot of mistakes, but the last thing I ever want to do is hurt you. I'm striving to become a better man, and I know I need to be honest with you about my past and the things I've struggled with. I'm glad that God will place you in my life. As we continue to grow in our relationship with Christ, I pray that God will prepare both of us for the marriage that is ahead. You are beautiful and amazing, and I can't wait to meet you someday and begin this journey with you.

After I read through the comments and answers, I was so inspired by the words of these men. They have sincere hearts, they think and pray for their future wives, and they want girls to protect their purity. Doesn't this give you hope for the future? I also want to take some time to tell you secrets about guys that shouldn't really be secrets.

1. Guys appreciate modesty. Even though this world tells women to be provocative and show off our bodies, godly men will be after a girl's heart, character, and personality.

2. Guys have their own definition of beauty. Godly men have very different views of beauty compared to worldly standards. Yes, some guys do like outward beauty, but they also look for girls who have a sense of humour, enjoy life, show humility, live out their calling for God, use their talents and gifts, and know that their value and worth is found in Christ.

3. Guys love a little mystery. A lot of guys are fascinated by the unknown and challenges. Most guys find it unattractive when girls "throw themselves" on them and become obsessive or clingy. Chase after God first and let the guy solve the mystery by coming after you.

4. Every guy you encounter is different and unique. There are so many guys out there! There are creative ones, studious one, imaginative ones, and the list goes on and on. We need to accept and be sensitive to every boy we encounter, whether as a friend or someone we love.

5. A guy's life does not revolve around girls. A godly man is not going to sit by his phone waiting for girls to call him, and he

will not be a "player." A true man after God's heart will be chasing after God first, before any girl comes into the picture. Here is another secret—guys love it when girls don't allow their lives to revolve around boys! So ladies, instead of waiting by your phones, enjoy life and today's moments; the guy will come in God's timing.

6. Guys are vulnerable. Have you heard the line that real men don't cry? Well, that's a complete myth. Guys, just like girls, are made in the image of God. They have the same emotions and feelings as anyone else. Don't play games with a guy's heart; instead, appreciate all that God has made him to be by being sensitive to his feelings and emotions.

7. Guys want to be the hero. God built into men the desire to be the conquerors, protectors, and providers. I'm a huge supporter of girl power and strength, but we have to let the guys be who God created them to be. The longing in a guy's heart to pursue the girl and win her is a reflection of God's heart.

So take heart, girls, there are still men out there who honour and respect woman who love and honour God. Remember that each one is unique, and you and I must be sensitive to them and let them live out their life to the fullest.

From My Heart to Yours

Ladies, if a guy ever tries to pressure you into something you're not comfortable with, he's not the one for you. If he tries to justify and manipulate his reasons, then he doesn't deserve you. If he tries to twist the Bible on you, then God is not truly in him. He will only damage your dignity and character in Christ. He will literally tear down your identity. As women of God, we're called to stand up and protect our sacred bodies. We're all worth so much more than someone else's schemes and lies, and we deserve the joy of the Lord.

Before I end this chapter, I want to remind you of something I have mentioned before, but I think is critical to remind you of here. God must be first, before any other boy comes into your life. This is tough to remember, but God's ways are best. His plans are good. It helps me to say this out loud: "God, I'd rather have you. I would rather have you." Trust me—he will be worth the wait.

The 10 Ways to Love:
LISTEN without interrupting
SHARE without pretending
SPEAK without judging
GIVE without wanting something in return
PRAY without giving up
ANSWER without quarrelling
ENJOY without complaining
TRUST without disloyalty
FORGIVE without condemning
PROMISE without forgetting

Be Empowered

Two are better than one, because they have a good return for their labor: if either of them falls down, one can help the other up. But pity anyone who falls and has no one to help them up. Also, if two lie down together, they will keep warm. But how can one keep warm alone? (Ecclesiastes 4:9–11)

"Above all else, guard your heart, for everything you do flows from it," (Proverbs 4:23).

"Resist the devil, and he will flee from you," (James 4:7b).

Flee from sexual immorality. All other sins a person commits are outside the body, but whoever sins sexually, sins against their own body. Do you not know that your bodies are temples of the Holy Spirit, who is in you, whom you have received from God? You are not your own; you were bought at a price. Therefore honor God with your bodies. (1 Corinthians 6:18–20)

Thought to Ponder

To the Girl who is Waiting for her Godly Man

By: Emily Sears

A relationship with a man will only be healthy if he's a godly man who respects and loves you and is not desensitized by this corrupt world in which we live. He should regularly read God's Word and practice what he preaches.

A woman who wants a godly man should look for certain qualities. He should be calm and not easily angered: "*If you stay calm you are wise, but if you have a hot temper, you only show how stupid you are,*" (Proverbs 14:29, GNT). As a woman of God, it's important to find someone who can collect his temper and keep his cool through trials and tribulations.

This godly man should be someone who can lead you to become a better lover of Jesus. I understand that not every man is destined to be a world leader, but I do believe that each individual man in this world has a leadership role to fulfill within a marriage.

This godly man should be prayerful. A man who doesn't pray doesn't truly have a relationship with the Lord. We should seek after someone who has a strong prayer life with the One who created him. A man worth pursuing is a man who seeks after God on a daily basis. Also, a prayerful man will encourage a prayerful relationship.

This godly man should have a good reputation: "*A good name is to be chosen rather than great riches, and favor is better than silver or gold,*" (Proverbs 22:1, ESV). While many people may not necessarily agree, I believe a God-fearing woman should desire to seek a man with a positive reputation. Everyone is entitled to their own opinion, but joining a man whose reputation is fallen is something you should think twice about before accepting. Seek to be with a man who gets compliments when his name is brought up in conversation.

We can conclude that any man who truly loves God is a man who loves without limitations. Women need to look for someone who is willing to showcase love no matter the circumstance. Most importantly, this godly man should be a loving man: "*But anyone who does not love does not know God, for God is love,*" (1 John 4:8, NLT).

To the Girl Waiting to Walk Down the Aisle
By: ANNALEE ROFFEL

As I'm writing this, I'm holding my baby boy and waiting for my husband to come home from work. Dating was amazing, but being married has changed my world. I thought I'd talk to you about what purity means to me, and how thankful I am that I saved my virginity for my husband. While I know a lot of you have struggled with this, I do hope a girl out there somewhere can feel some hope today. Purity while dating is such a hard thing amidst the temptations of our world. Everywhere we look there are temptations—magazines while standing in line at the grocery store, TV shows, even strangers walking along the street.

"If everyone else is having sex before marriage or crossing the line, why can't I?"

Because you're a child of God. Your body is not your own! God made sex, and it's a beautiful thing, but it was not made for just anyone to participate in. It's made for a marriage between a husband and wife. By saving sex for marriage, you're not only obeying God, you're also saving yourself a lot of hassle. Every person you sleep with prior to marriage takes a little part of your purity; I wanted to protect my virginity, and you can too. Don't let this scare you if you've had sex outside of marriage. God sent his only son, because he loved us so much, to die for our sins. To take our sins upon Himself. If we repent, we are forgiven because of God's grace. No sin is bigger than another, but, dear sister, you are worth more than a one-night stand; you are worth more than a guy not remembering your name; you are worth more than that! Save yourself to be loved properly by a godly man. Save your purity!

chapter twelve

What Is Your Story?

*There will never be another woman who owns the
look, the personality, and the experience that you do.
Those ingredients make up the recipe
that defines who you are, and it's your
gift from the Lord—own it.*[21]
CANDACE CAMERON BURE

MY GREATEST FEAR USED TO BE SPEAKING IN FRONT OF PEOPLE. I
remember this all throughout my high school years. Fear overwhelmed
me deep into my core. I was not only fearful, but I would sweat in
places I did not know a person could sweat in. I would get hives over
my face and neck, and my throat would close up to the point where
it was hard to breathe. What made it even worse was that everyone
knew how nervous and self-conscious I was. I remember the last time
this happened. I left the classroom praying to God: *God, you have to
take this fear away from me. I don't want to live in fear of speaking in
front of others.*

In the twelfth grade, I took an acting course, which helped me
overcome this fear. I was on stage almost every week, having to "get
into character" and perform in front of my fellow classmates. I hated

it at first, but it helped to bring me to a point in my life where now I don't even become afraid before speaking in front of people. God heard me that day in the school hallway.

Your Story Is Important

Everyone has a story to tell. The way God designed every single human being is so extraordinary and indescribable. No other woman on this planet has your personality, your passion, or your story. This is a precious gift from God directly to you, so own it! God needs you to tell your story, and only you can tell it. I had to ask God to help me overcome my deepest fear, because I knew if I was to live a life of following Him, I'd need to learn how to speak to people. You see, telling our testimony to others is essential when we follow Christ.

It's important for you to know your story and develop your testimony. A testimony is your story of how you came to know Christ and how He is still working in your life: "*Always be prepared to give an answer to everyone who asks you to give the reason for the hope that you have. But do this with gentleness and respect,*" (1 Peter 3:15).

We must be ready and prepared for that time when someone asks us why we love Jesus. Here are some steps to developing a testimony:

1. Describe your life before Jesus.
2. Describe how you came to know Jesus.
3. Describe the difference He has made in your life.
4. Describe what God is still doing in your life.
5. Practice saying your testimony out loud.
6. Be real; don't be afraid to share your weaknesses.

Developing a testimony can take a long time. The kind of testimony outlined above is good for when you're giving a testimony at a church event, Bible study, or worship night. However, we also need to have a testimony ready that we can say in less than two minutes.

For instance, if you're in an elevator with someone and they ask you about your faith, you probably only have the amount of time you're in the elevator to tell them about Jesus. You can't say your ten-minute testimony you used at church last Sunday. It's vital and critical that you summarize your testimony for when times like this arise.

Here are the steps to making a three minute or less testimony:

1. Talk about a recent issue where God helped you overcome.
2. Talk about a life lesson that God helped you learn.
3. Use an everyday experience when you felt God's presence or when He spoke to you.
4. Practice saying your story out loud with a timer.
5. Be sensitive and be real.

Always remember that it is God who is working through you. You don't bring someone to Christ; God does this through His Holy Spirit: "*For I am not ashamed of this Good News about Christ. It is the power of God at work, saving everyone who believes,*" (Romans 1:16, NLT). You can tell your story and tell people all about Jesus, but they have to decide for themselves whom they will serve. Never let yourself become self-righteous just because you allowed God to use you to bring someone to Christ. Stay humble. Show empathy. Be compassionate. Be patient. Stay focused on God. Never be ashamed of your story. Never be afraid to tell it.

And never apologize for loving Jesus.

Actions Speak Louder Than Words

Your testimony is more than just speaking about your story; it's in your actions every single day. This life is a mission field, and you are in it. We aren't meant to sit on the sidelines; we're meant for action.

Think about the following scenarios. You see garbage on the ground on your way to the coffee shop. Do you walk by it, or do you pick it up to throw out? You see an old man drop his grocery bag. Do you help him, or do you just stand there? You see how stressed the bank clerk is. Do you say something encouraging, or do you become impatient and rude? What do you do if you realize the cashier has given you too much change back by mistake? When your friend is stressed and hurting, do you comfort her, or do you put your own needs ahead of hers?

I know you're not perfect. I know it can be hard to be Christ-like every single minute of every single day, but we never know when an unbeliever may be watching us. We must be conscious of the way we put our witness into action.

Become a Servant

The best way to put our witness into action is to become a servant. Matthew tells us that Jesus didn't come to this world to be served, but to serve. I suggest you open your Bibles to John 13 to read about this:

> *It was just before the Passover Festival. Jesus knew that the hour had come for him to leave this world and go to the Father. Having loved his own who were in the world, he loved them to the end ... so he got up from the meal, took off his outer clothing, and wrapped a towel around his waist. After that, he poured water into a basin and began to wash his disciples' feet, drying them with the towel that was wrapped around him. He came to Simon Peter, who said to him, "Lord, are you going to wash my feet?"*
>
> *Jesus replied, "You do not realize now what I am doing, but later you will understand."*
>
> *"No," said Peter, "you shall never wash my feet."*
>
> *Jesus answered, "Unless I wash you, you have no part with me."* (John 13:1, 4–8)

This story paints a beautiful picture of true humbleness and selflessness. I don't know about you, but that's the way I want to live.

Here are some steps to becoming true servants:

1. Start thinking of others as more important than yourself.
2. Base your identity in Christ.
3. Concentrate on what you're doing and don't compare yourself to other Christians.
4. Pay attention.
5. Be available and take every opportunity.
6. Stay focused on Jesus.

Becoming God's servant and putting our testimony into action is not an overnight thing. We can't expect it to come right away. Be patient with yourself and always do your best. Start practicing some of these techniques slowly over the next few weeks, and soon they'll become part of your everyday character.

Become a Mentor

As you go through this journey called life, you'll always be learning and refining your story. Along the way, it's good for you to pass what you've learned on to someone else. You need to be mentoring someone under you. This means that you don't just tell a person your life story once and walk away, but you walk alongside of them. Train and mentor them in the way so that they will be stronger and wiser than you were at their age. You can also learn from people you mentor. Even though they're younger than you, they still have the same Holy Spirit working in their life.

Here are some tips for sharing your testimony in a mentoring situation:

1. Build a trusting relationship.
2. Encourage them in all aspects of life.

3. Share personal stories.
4. Believe in them.
5. Love them. Don't just pretend to love them, but genuinely love and care for them in the same way God loves you.
6. Listen. Don't just talk and tell them what to do, but let them voice their opinions and share their story.
7. Never give up.

Say It with Love

Everyone experiences God differently. Your story may be very different than that of your best friend, neighbour, or co-worker. It's critical that you tell your story with sensitivity and love. Paul writes about this: "*Instead, we will speak the truth in love, growing in every way more and more like Christ, who is the head of his body, the church*," (Ephesians 4:15, NLT).

Jesus Christ was the greatest example of this while He was here on earth. He could have walked around condemning everyone to hell, but instead He shared the Good News with love and gentleness. Take a look at how Jesus confronted the woman at the well in John 4.

> *Now Jesus learned that the Pharisees had heard that he was gaining and baptizing more disciples than John—although in fact it was not Jesus who baptized, but his disciples. So he left Judea and went back once more to Galilee. Now he had to go through Samaria. So he came to a town in Samaria called Sychar … and Jesus, tired as he was from the journey, sat down by the well. It was about noon. When a Samaritan woman came to draw water, Jesus said to her, "Will you give me a drink?" (His disciples had gone into the town to buy food.)*
>
> *The Samaritan woman said to him, "You are a Jew and I am a Samaritan woman. How can you ask me for a drink?" (For Jews do not associate with Samaritans.)*

Jesus answered her, "If you knew the gift of God and who it is that asks you for a drink, you would have asked him and he would have given you living water."

"Sir," the woman said, "you have nothing to draw with and the well is deep. Where can you get this living water? Are you greater than our father Jacob, who gave us the well and drank from it himself, as did also his sons and his livestock?"

Jesus answered, "Everyone who drinks this water will be thirsty again, but whoever drinks the water I give them will never thirst. Indeed, the water I give them will become in them a spring of water welling up to eternal life."

The woman said to him, "Sir, give me this water so that I won't get thirsty and have to keep coming here to draw water."

He told her, "Go, call your husband and come back."

"I have no husband," she replied.

Jesus said to her, "You are right when you say you have no husband. The fact is, you have had five husbands, and the man you now have is not your husband. What you have just said is quite true."

"Sir," the woman said, "I can see that you are a prophet. Our ancestors worshiped on this mountain, but you Jews claim that the place where we must worship is in Jerusalem."

"Woman," Jesus replied, "believe me, a time is coming when you will worship the Father neither on this mountain nor in Jerusalem. You Samaritans worship what you do not know; we worship what we do know, for salvation is from the Jews. Yet a time is coming and has now come when the true worshipers will worship the Father in the Spirit and in truth, for they are the kind of worshipers the Father seeks. God is spirit, and his worshipers must worship in the Spirit and in truth."

The woman said, "I know that Messiah (called Christ) is
coming. When he comes, he will explain everything to us."
Then Jesus declared, "I, the one speaking to you—I am he."

Oh, every time I read this passage, I'm overwhelmed with joy
for the love Jesus has for all His people. Did you notice the way Jesus
witnessed and told His story to the lost woman? This Samaritan
woman was despised and viewed as an outcast by many. She was
adulterous and living in sin. God didn't start off preaching the Word
to her; instead, He first built her trust. Here we see that God's news
is for everyone, no matter where they come from. God sat at the well
and spoke with patience and gentleness. He didn't condemn or judge,
He just asked her questions, letting her share her story too. After
Jesus built some trust, He told her about God's gift through love. Did
you notice how Jesus ended the conversation? He didn't force her to
believe; He gave her the freedom to choose. In the same way, you and
I must always tell our story with love.

Never Stop Learning

Even when you've developed your testimony, become a mentor, and
told an unbeliever about your faith, your story is never finished. I
want to encourage you to never stop learning. Never put a limit on
where God can take you, or what He can show you. A woman after
God's own heart knows that she can never stop growing in Christ.
Don't be the girl who has put a box around her life. Don't just stand
there, never moving, and just staying the same. Love God and tell
people about Him. Keep looking to Jesus; gaze upon Him.

I don't mean to say I am perfect. I haven't learned all I should
even yet, but I keep working toward that day when I will finally
be all that Christ saved me for and wants me to be. No, dear

brothers, I'm still not all I should be ... (Philippians 3:12–13, TLB)

Every morning when you wake up, be the girl who asks God to show you what you can learn and what He has to show you. For me, I never want to stop. Even when I reach those golden gates of heaven, I know God will have work for me to still do. God is not done with you yet.

It Is a Privilege

Always remember that it's privilege to be part of God's message to the world. Your story may seem insignificant to you, but it could bring someone to Christ. Telling others about Christ is the most amazing thing you can do on this earth. You plant the seed, and God will help it grow. You may even see someone come to Jesus through your words, and that is the best feeling in the world.

Even though you're the one telling the story, God is the one who is saving them. God and His Holy Spirit will use you by planting the seed in someone's heart. You can't make the decision for them; instead, become patient and allow the work of God to take over. You're helping grow the Kingdom in heaven. When you tell your story, I believe the angels and God Himself dance and cheer you on. Can you imagine? I'm getting goosebumps and tears as I write this. You and I have the power to tell the truth about life or death. Will you do it? Will you help grow the Kingdom?

As you grow and mature in Christ, telling your story will become a natural part of your daily life. The only thing from this life we can bring into heaven are people.

Survival Tips from My Heart to Yours

This life can be hard, and living out our story for God every day has its challenges. I hope and pray you allow God to continue to write your story as you live out your days for Him. Here are my survival tips:

1. Set your heart on God.
2. Journey with friends.
3. Delight in God's love.
4. Reach out to the lost.
5. Have a thankful heart.
6. Make worship and praise your lifestyle.
7. Listen, pay attention, and let the Holy Spirit be active in your life.
8. Speak out; do not be silent.
9. Take yourself seriously; be all of who God created you to be.
10. Live in the presence of God and in the hope of eternal life.

Be Empowered

Therefore go and make disciples of all nations, baptizing them in the name of the Father and of the Son and of the Holy Spirit, and teaching them to obey everything I have commanded you. And surely I am with you always, to the very end of the age. (Matthew 28:19–20)

"And how will anyone go and tell them without being sent? That is why the scriptures say, 'How beautiful are the feet of messengers who bring good news!'" (Romans 10:15).

"Let all the world look to me for salvation! For I am God; there is no other," (Isaiah 45:22, NLT).

"Do your best to present yourself to God as one approved, a workman who does not need to be ashamed and who correctly handles the word of truth," (2 Timothy 2:15).

Thought to Ponder
To the Girl Who Is Radical for Jesus
By: Corisa Miller

We live in a broken world filled with darkness and despair. Thankfully, because of the greatest sacrifice ever known to man, there is a light in our lives that never stops shining. I'm not saying that just because we believe in Jesus the world won't feel dark and broken … because it can still feel that way … but it all depends on how we look at the situation. Do you look at your struggles and still thank God for everything? Or do you run as far as you can from Him? During your struggles, do you seek Him in everything you do and share the Word? Or do you hide from your faith, because you're afraid of what the world may think of you? The Bible tells us: "*Do not be afraid; keep on speaking, do not be silent,*" (Acts 18:9).

Are you afraid to show your faith, or are you ready to go out and be a radical disciple of Christ? God doesn't want us to be ashamed of our faith, but to stand firm in our faith and share the Word with everyone, wherever we go. We are called to be a light in the world and live radically for Him!

The Oxford online dictionary definition of radical is "Characterized by departure from tradition; innovative or progressive." It also means to favour or effecting extreme or revolutionary changes, as in political organizations. These are all examples of the extreme radicalism Jesus brought to the people of His time. His love was authentic and extreme. His message to the people, and the miracles He performed, have inspired and moved generations. Jesus carried all of our burdens and died so that we could be set free! He is the true example of radicalism. Jesus brought change to the entire world, changing the hearts and minds of nations.

In order to be radical for Jesus, we need to stop stressing over the things we can't control and fully let God take over every part of our lives. We must live out God's commandments and be an example to others. We must share God's Word everywhere we go and focus our minds on things above. We must not be afraid, and we must not be silent. We must speak about Jesus, not just with our church friends, but with everyone! We must be willing to stand and defend what we believe. We must go out into the world, preserve the goodness, and be a light in this dark world:

You are the salt of the earth. But if the salt loses its saltiness, how can it be made salty again? It is no longer good for anything, except to be thrown out and trampled underfoot. You are the light of the world. A town built on a hill cannot be hidden. Neither do people light a lamp and put it under a bowl. Instead they put it on its stand, and it gives light to everyone in the house. In the same way, let your light shine before others, that they may see your good deeds and glorify your Father in heaven. (Matthew 5:13–16)

Are you ready to go and be a light in the world? Are you ready to show His unfailing love to everyone? Live radically for Him.

chapter thirteen

Run the Race
Heavenward

Heaven just gets closer and closer each day. [22]
AMY GRANT

BREATHE IN. BREATHE OUT. FEEL THAT? THAT'S LIFE. YOUR LIFE. GOD gave it to you. What are you going to do with it?

For me, it all goes back to the mountains of Colorado. As I think about how magnificent and beautiful they were, my heart feels warm and grateful to God for bringing me to where I am today. He stirred something deep in my heart that day, and I'm living it out as I write these words. I remember starring at those mountains, with the sun shining down, wondering what heaven would be like when I get to see my magnificent Creator face to face. Surely there is more to life than the here-and-now.

Have you ever stopped to think about heaven or eternity? I mean really think about it. Eternity is forever. Heaven is forever. Just think … you and I are made to live forever. I used to be a person who wanted to create a legacy here on earth. I think we can all be guilty of that. Who can blame us? Our society tells us to believe in the here-and-now. Our culture teaches us to always put ourselves first, and our world is seriously blinded to the truth that God made us to last forever.

When you come to the realization that you could live forever, everything changes. Your values change, your priorities change, and even your general outlook on life changes. Instead of chasing after a legacy on earth, you'll start running towards the gates of heaven. Everything on this earth will soon pass away. Our titles, money, and possessions will all fade, but God remains forever. The Bible says that God's plans endure forever; His purposes last eternally. And guess what? You and I are a part of that glorious unfolding.

Eternity is defined as a deep and abiding awareness of something beyond our borders. You see, God has planted eternity inside each one of us. I want to start living in light of eternity. Rick Warren says in his book, *The Purpose Driven Life*, that when we get closer to God, everything else will become small.[23] In 1 John 2:17, we read, *"This world is fading away, along with everything that people crave. But anyone who does what pleases God will live forever,"* (NLT).

Just the other day, I was having a conversation with a friend about how faith impacts our lives. We were talking about health and how to prevent Alzheimer's and cancer. She told me what precautions she uses to help prevent these diseases, but she also said something that was critical: "Yes, I may get cancer, and if I do, so be it. I will work hard to prevent it now, but I am not afraid of it. I know that after this life I go to heaven to be with my God, so I have nothing to fear." I knew this truth, but once it was said out loud I finally understood it. Have you ever thought about life this way?

This life is also a preparation for heaven. We must not waste it. When we meet God, I believe He will ask us two questions. The first will be, "What did you do with my Son, Jesus Christ?" You and I are called to live a life that pleases God. We must show others we love God by the way we live. I also believe God will ask us, "What did you do with the gifts and talents I gave you?" God wants us to use our gifts and what He has given us for His glory and to help build the Kingdom. I hope this doesn't scare you, but excites you.

The way you live today impacts eternity! Life is beautiful! This life is to be taken seriously, but I know that God is a creative and imaginative God who takes delight when we enjoy His creation. Scripture says that there is more in store for us than we can even imagine right now! Enjoy and love the life God has given you. Embrace every part of it.

I can't promise you a life of perfect peace, but I can promise you that, with God, you will have the most abundant joy. It's a joy that is born deep in your soul when you rise above this world and choose God instead. Being joy-filled means that you will still have to work hard and endure tough times, but you will also find that your worth and reason to live come through Christ alone.

The truth is simple—this world is not our home. We are simply passing through. With Christ, you and I are citizens of heaven … and heaven just gets closer and closer each day. Jesus, our King, will be coming back again. In a moment, everyone will fall silent. In a moment, Jesus will claim His citizens of heaven. In a moment, every knee will bow and tongue will confess that He is Lord of Lords. Oh, what a glorious day that will be! I want to put my trust and hope in the God who is the same yesterday, today, and tomorrow.

Can you imagine what it will be like to meet Jesus face-to-face? Will you live in light of eternity? I don't know about you, but I plan on living forever.

The Importance of Time

Time—there never seems to be enough of it. Sometimes it feels like the weeks fly by, while other days can feel like an eternity. I'm only twenty-three years old, but I feel like the days, months, and years are going faster and faster and won't ever slow down. Time is the one thing about this life we can never stop; it will always keep moving. Sometimes I just wish that for a second we could freeze time. Just sit and reflect on all that has happened. As daughters of the King, we must value our time. The psalmist says, "*Teach us to number our days, that we may get a heart of wisdom*," (Psalm 90:12).

"*Look carefully then how you* [live]*, not as unwise but as wise, making the best use of the time, because the days are evil*," (Ephesians 5:15–17, ESV). This verse is referring to more than just a daily devotion, a one minute prayer, or a worship song. This is about working hard at everything we do. It's about including God in every aspect of our being, and trying to do our best to help win people for the Kingdom of God. I urge you to value time. Remember, heaven is getting closer each day.

Run the Race Invitation:
You are a child of God.
Your purpose in life is to live to always praise God in your words, thoughts, and deeds.
You are born to lead. You are born to make a difference in this world.
You are invited to make God higher than life itself.
Do not love this world; instead, give it up and do anything God asks you to do.
Be Ready. Be on your guard.
Live for the audience of the One.
Every day, do not get up until you have bent your knees to the Lord, surrendering your mind, soul, and body for God to take and use.
Do not give up. Endure the pain. Always remember God's truths.

> Run the race heavenward so that when you enter the heavenly gates, God will say you to, "Well done, good and faithful servant. You are home."

Do It All for God's Glory

God made the universe. He made everything—you, me, the sky, the ocean, the trees, and everything in its place. Everything was made by God, and everything reflects Him. The birds sing praises to Him, the waves of the oceans speak His name, and even the highest mountain tops glorify Him. You and I were made to do the same.

> *Work hard to prove that you really are among those God has called and chosen. Do these things, and you will never fall away. Then God will give you a <u>grand entrance into the eternal kingdom</u> of our Lord and Savior Jesus Christ.* (2 Peter 1:10–11, NLT, emphasis added)

We were created to bring God glory. How do we do this? We bring God glory when we love Him above ourselves. We bring Him glory when we do everything in His name, and love Him first. This whole life happens because it's not about us. Living for God's glory is fun, joyful, and the best way to live.

I'm asking you to think critically about your life, surrender it all to God, and run the race heavenward.

> *Do you not know that in a race all the runners run, but only one gets the prize? Run in such a way as to get the prize. Everyone who competes in the games goes into strict training. They do it to*

get a crown that will not last, but we do it to get a crown that will last forever. (1 Corinthians 9:24–25)

What will you do when you first enter the gates of heaven and see Jesus face to face? I can only imagine what it will be like when I enter the gates of heaven and see my Lord face to face for the first time. I may bow, I may shake, or I may run into the arms of Jesus. Whatever the cost, from this day until eternity, I will be with Him forever.

God wants the whole world to know about His grace, truth, and love. We are simply strings in His grand masterpiece. Will you do your part in His grand masterpiece?

Many people will mess up today with yesterday. They will re-think and over-analyze. They will bring up yesterday's letdowns and failures. Then bitterness, resentment, and regret will destroy what could have been a wonderful day. You see, every day is a new page to your story.

I have shared with you a lot of my secrets. My last secret is simply this: whatever is done in love is done well. This is a big, big world, and you're living in it. Isn't it amazing how God created the stars and moon and holds the whole earth in place, yet He looked at you and me and thought to create us too?

Oh, precious sisters and daughters of the King, I hope you have been inspired to embrace your inner beauty and find your identity in God. Before I leave you, I want to share with you the last important steps in this journey. I learned these principles from Rick Warren's book, *Purpose Driven Life*. I hope they help you as you go continue to grow in the Lord.

I hope you are ready for the journey ahead. It will be a long one, with many battles, trials, and heartaches, but it will also be a time of celebration, excitement, and joy. I believe together we can be the change this world needs. Now that you know your beauty mark rests in Christ alone, I want you to go and live out that truth. Tell other girls. Admire their beauty. Stand up for what is right. Love wild. Run free. I am so excited for how you will impact God's kingdom.

There are no shortcuts to God. There are no bargains or cutbacks to finding our identity in Christ. The adventure of embracing everything God has to offer us can never be rushed. While this world is always concerned about how fast we grow, God is concerned about how strong, durable, and tough we become. Remember when I talked about how our fruit of the Spirit will take time to ripen? That's what God will do with your life. As you continue to walk in His ways, He will gradually ripen you to be all He created you to be. Psalm 32:8, 10 says: "*I will guide you along the best pathway for your life. I will advise you and watch over you … unfailing love surrounds all those who trust in the Lord,*" (NLT).

I encourage you to slow down in all areas of your life. Slow down and focus on what God is saying to you today. At the same time, press on for the hope of what He still has in store for you. We all have both pain and joy ahead, so don't become discouraged.

But these things I plan won't happen right away. Slowly, steadily, surely, the time approaches when the vision will be fulfilled. If it seems slow, do not despair, for these things will surely come to pass. Just be patient! They will not be overdue a single day! (Habakkuk 2:3, TLB)

There is so much more to your life than what you see now. I pray and hope you let God lead you down the path He has marked for you. "*No eye has seen, no ear has heard, and no mind has imagined what God has prepared for those who love him,*" (1 Corinthians 2:9, NLT).

Oh, dear sisters, you are worth so much more than settling for what this world calls beautiful. You deserve to know you are adorned by the King, the Creator of the universe, the one who knew you before you were born. You are His daughter and forever cherished by the King. It's time for you to cherish and embrace your inner beauty the way God does.

Lastly, I want to share with you my favourite scripture passage, Psalm 63. Every time I read these words, God shows me something new. This is my daily prayer to my Lord as a reminder that I am beautiful and precious in His sight. It also serves to remind me to run the race heavenward, for God is my joy, deep in my soul. May your life bring Him praise for the rest of your days, until He calls you home.

You, God are my God, earnestly I seek you;
I thirst for you, my whole being longs for you,
in a dry and parched land where there is no water.
I have seen you in the sanctuary and beheld your power and
your glory.
Because your love is better than life, my lips will glorify you.
I will praise you as long as I live, and in your name I will lift
up my hands.
I will be fully satisfied as with the richest of foods; with singing
lips my mouth will praise you.
On my bed I remember you; I think of you through the watches
of the night.
Because you are my help, I sing in the shadow of your wings.
I cling to you; your right hand upholds me. (Psalm 63:1–8)

Just in case you forgot, your future is in God's hands, so walk strong, girl. Love who God has made you to be. Love others the way God loves you. And never stop embracing your inner beauty.

Today, I'm asking you to step out in boldness and be brave. And start spreading the love.

Remember, God's mercies are new every morning.

And today is a new page.

So start writing.

Breathe in. Breathe out. Feel that? That's life. Your life. God gave it to you. What are you going to do with it?

Be Empowered

When troubles of any kind come your way, consider it an opportunity for great joy. For you know that when your faith is tested, your endurance has a chance to grow ... God blesses those who patiently endure testing and temptation. (James 1:2–3, 12a, NLT)

"Then Jesus declared, 'I am the bread of life. Whoever comes to me will never go hungry, and whoever believes in me will never be thirsty,'" (John 6:35).

"In the same way that You gave Me a mission in the world, I give them a mission in the world," (John 17:18, MSG).

I have fought the good fight, I have finished the race, I have kept the faith. Henceforth there is laid up for me the crown of righteousness, which the Lord, the righteous judge, will award to me on that day, and not only to me but also to all who have loved his appearing. (2 Timothy 4:7–9, ESV)

epilogue

To the Girl Who Is Ruled by Doubt and Anxiety: You Can Dance in the Rain

THERE IS A SCRIPTURE VERSE ON MY MIRROR. I SEE IT EVERY DAY. IT says, "*Do not be anxious about anything, but in every situation, by prayer and petition … present your requests to God. And the peace of God … will guard your hearts and minds …*" (Philippians 4:6–7). Reading it is easy. Living and believing that truth is the hard part. Yes, I believe God will take care of me. Yes, I believe God holds my future. So why is it so easy to let anxiety and fear corrupt my mind?

To the girl who is ruled by doubt and worry—this one is for you.

Worry and doubt do not come from God. God wants us to be filled with hope, faith, love, and excitement to live life! Unfortunately, this world is far from perfect, and with one little touch of rain, it can send us spiralling out of control.

God is the father of light, and Satan is the father of lies. Worry and doubt are lies that Satan tries to plant in our minds to take our focus off God. Maybe you're stressed about getting into the "right" university. Maybe you put too much pressure on yourself to be "better." Maybe you're worn out from the weight of this world. Or maybe you just don't know how you're going to pay all the bills this month. Whatever it is, you are not alone.

Jeremiah 29:11 is one of my favourite verses. We've all heard it a thousand times, but in its simplicity, I want to share it with you again: "*'For I know the plans I have for you,' says the Lord. 'They are plans for good and not for disaster, to give you a future and a hope.'*" (NLT). The following three verses hold the underlying key: "*In those days when you pray, I will listen. If you look for me wholeheartedly, you will find me ... I will end your captivity and restore your fortunes,*" (Jeremiah 29:11–14).

There is a two-fold truth here. You and I must remember that there is hope for tomorrow, because God holds our future. However, we must also continue to search for Him wholeheartedly. What does this mean exactly? Our hearts are vulnerable. Our hearts want to worship something, and if it's not God, it's something of the world. We must dethrone the world and replace it with God's truth and light.

Instead of letting doubt and worry rule our mind, we pray, pray, pray. Instead of letting the father of lies dictate our thoughts, we fill our minds with truth from God's Word. Instead of surrounding ourselves with negative things, we sing songs of praise. And we learn to dance in the rain.

'Cause, beautiful girl, you will get through the hard things. One twirl at a time.

Even through the worst of storms, you can choose joy, peace, patience, love, and hope, because we know God's ways are best and true. We believe that God will calm the storm.

Allow God to break apart the lies of doubt and worry. Allow God to steady your heart. Soon, you will learn to love life again. You will start to see beauty in the people and nature all around you. You will start to see a reason to live. Most importantly, you will start to see yourself through His eyes.

Girl, you are a treasure. You are loved. You are precious in His eyes.

Today, I choose to be the girl who is not ruled by worry and doubt.

I choose to walk in His light.

I choose to run wild.

I choose to love free.

I choose to dance in the rain.

Will you join me?

study guide
and Group Discussion Questions

THIS BOOK CAN BE READ INDIVIDUALLY OR WITH A GROUP. I'M A HUGE believer in the power of numbers and the fact that we can all learn from each other. If you are reading this book for a Bible study or with a group of friends, here are some discussion questions and challenges for each chapter.

Before you begin this Bible study, there are some things I want to make sure you know. I pray this can be a group where girls come together in the presence of God. I hope you can build a safe place where everyone can speak openly, knowing they can trust the group. I encourage you to take the risk and be vulnerable and open about your struggles and trials to learn from one another. Before each chapter study, I encourage you take the time to pray for one another and include God in everything.

Chapter 1: Created for so Much More Than an Ordinary Life

Question 1: What does Acts 17:28 mean when it says, "*For in Him we live and move and have our being*"? Discuss as a group.

Question 2: Are you someone who thinks you have no purpose in life? Are you busy saying "me, me, me" instead of, "God's way, God's way, God's way"? How can you change your perspective?

How can you help a friend who doesn't know they have purpose in life? Share with the group.

Question 3: What does it mean to represent Christ?

Question 4: What does inner beauty mean to you? Every person in the group needs to write out a list of what inner beauty means to them. I challenge you to go back into God's Word to discover how inner beauty starts with Him. Discuss openly or write a list for yourself.

Question 5: I shared with you my belief that beauty is something God has planted inside of us all. Re-read Psalm 139 and say it out loud, inserting your name in each of the "I's." What does this Scripture passage say about your beauty and worth in Christ?

Question 6: What is your favourite Scripture passage? What is it about that passage that helps you know your worth is found in Christ alone? You can either share with the group or keep this as a personal reminder.

Chapter 2: An Identity Crisis

Question 1: What's holding you back from saying "yes" to God? What's holding you back from making God your foundation? Share openly with the group.

Question 2: Read Genesis 3:5–7. Why does this world have an identity crisis? Read 1 Corinthians 3:11. Why is a foundation so important? How can you help this world come back to the way God first intended it to be? Brainstorm with your group.

Question 3: I explained to you who God is to me. He is my peace, my rest, my strength, and my comfort. Who is God to you? Remember not to make God into your own image, but to find out who He is through Scripture. Write out your own description of God and what He means to you.

Question 4: What is the Holy Spirit's main job? Why is He here on earth with us?

Question 5: Salvation is critical to following Jesus Christ. If there is someone in the group who does not yet know Jesus, spend some time on this subject. Don't rush it, but openly discuss how you came to Christ and why He is so important in your life. A word of caution—do not try to force your friend to be saved. She must decide for herself. Instead, speak words of wisdom, a prayer, and let her know you're there if she has any more questions. Make sure you also follow up and stay in contact with her. Does your group know someone who isn't saved? Take some time to pray for that individual.

Question 6: Before God made this world, He saw a vision of His people on earth. He chose you. He loves you. What does that mean to you? Re-read the chart "Lost Identity vs. Completely His." What does this tell you?

Question 7: Read Ephesians 4:23, Romans 12:3, and 1 Peter 3:9. What is God trying to say to you about forgiveness? Why is it sometimes hard to forgive? Why is it important to forgive others?

Chapter 3: Making Him the Centre of It All

Question 1: Worship is not something we just do on Sundays or when we're singing our favourite praise song. Worship is a lifestyle. How can you worship God in everything you do? Discuss with the group and be specific. How do you express worship?

Question 2: We need to practice His presence. We all need solitude, silence, and surrender in our lives to draw closer to God. Discuss with the group a plan of action to make this possible. For example, when I want to practice His presence and have solitude, I turn off all my technology and go for a big hike. This is an individual assignment, but talk about how you can go about doing this.

Question 3: Just because we're Christians doesn't mean we're immune to sin and temptation. It's everywhere. Explain to the group a time you were tempted and how you dealt with it. Encourage one another.

Question 4: Read Jeremiah 29:13 and Romans 10:17. How do we follow God in His truth?

Question 5: We serve a faithful God. Through the storm and through the calm, I want to trust in God. Do you? Read 1 Peter 4:12 and Mathew 14:22–36. Discuss with the group how you can trust God more instead of relying on your own strength. Take courage and walk on the water too.

Question 6: Read Romans 12:4–10. Why is it so important to be committed to your church? Discuss with the group how you serve God through your church. If you're not active in your church, how can you start today?

Question 7: Read Hebrew 2:1–4. I have given you eight steps to help keep you from drifting away. What are some other helpful tips to add to this list? How do you plan on drawing close to God today?

Chapter 4: A Holy Temple

Question 1: Read 1 Corinthians 16:18–20. What does it mean to have a holy temple? What does it mean to glorify God with your body?

Question 2: Explain your own definition of body image. Discuss openly with the group your opinions on clothing and modesty. How can you dress to show you love Jesus? Why is it important? What are your struggles and insecurities?

Question 3: What does "a virtuous woman" mean to you? Go back and read Proverbs 31:10–26.

Question 4: Go ahead and open your Bibles to read each characteristic of how God sees you. When you're finished reading all of those texts, pray and ask God to help you see your body the way He does. Pray for each other.

Question 5: Read Jeremiah 17:7–8 and 1 Samuel 16:7. What does it mean when it says "God looks at our hearts"?

Question 6: As women, we are always comparing ourselves to others. I shared with you my questions that help me remember that my worth is found in Christ alone. What kind of strategies can you come up with that remind you to accept the person God made you to be? How can you stop comparing yourself to others?

Question 7: How can technology be dangerous to our bodies? How do you view technology? I challenge you to try out the exercise in this chapter. Can you choose God over technology?

Question 8: In what ways can you speak justice, love mercy, and walk humbly? Refer back to the chapter and re-read the verse to help you.

Chapter 5: This Thing Called "Beauty"

Question 1: How do you define your own beauty—by the world or through God's Word?

Question 2: Make up your own definition of beauty. Use Scripture and your own life experiences.

Question 3: What is your relationship with the scale and your weight? Do you obsess over it? Do you love the skin and body God gave you? How can you love you for you?

Question 4: Taking good care of our bodies by eating right and exercising gives honour and glory to God. Have you ever thought about it this way before? How can you honour God in this way?

Question 5: How do you deal with vanity in a self-absorbed world?

Question 6: Beauty is all around us. What can you do to encourage other people's beauty?

Question 7: What does it mean to reflect our Creator? How does He become our beauty mark?

Question 8: Imperfections are there to keep us humble and focused on God. How can you own your imperfections? How can you see past your flaws and still have purpose for living?

Chapter 6: Leave a Legacy of Grace, Part I

Question 1: The tongue is one of the most powerful things God gave us. It can either speak life or death. Think deeply about your own words and what you've said throughout today. If we're honest, there are two sides to every person—a side that's loving, encouraging, and full of positivity, and a side that can be impatient, rude, and selfish. Think for a moment how you use your words. How can you speak life instead of death?

Question 2: Through Scripture we see how words direct our path and can have consequences. Has there been a time in your life when you said something that you regret because you hurt someone? How did/can you deal with it? How can you learn from these consequences?

Question 3: Gossip is destructive, damaging, and dangerous. With girls, gossip can become contagious and addictive to the point where we don't even realize we're doing it. Brainstorm with the group some strategies to stop the gossip. How amazing it would be if your study group started a chain reaction of stopping the gossip!

Question 4: You have the power to speak life into your own life. So many of us are our own worst enemy. It's time to train your mind and heart. Refer back to the steps I gave you from this chapter. How can you get rid of negative self-talk?

Question 5: How is silence a gift? How can you guard your words and think before you speak?

Question 6: How can you let your words be an example to unbelievers and other believers? What does it mean when I say that our words tell others about our relationship with God?

Question 7: How does self-control relate to leaving a legacy of grace?

Chapter 7: Leave a Legacy of Grace, Part II

Question 1: We all have emotions. God created emotions to be good. How are emotions good? Give some examples. How can our emotions turn bad? Is anger good or bad? Go back and re-read the scripture that tells us how God wants us to deal with anger.

Question 2: How does whining and complaining impact your life? How do the feelings of shame, guilt, and regret impact your life? Be honest and open with the group. Discuss how you can move forward into God's radiant light. How can you become a new creation and change? Go back and read the passage in Colossians.

Question 3: Are meltdowns okay? How do you deal with all your emotions cooped up inside? Do you let them hurt everyone around you? Share a story with the group. Maybe some of you have something that needs to be talked out. Support one another and remember to rise above it.

Question 4: How can God help you with stress? How do we change our attitudes and thoughts so we can still honour God with our emotions?

Question 5: How can you change your perspective? Re-read Ephesians 5:1–2 (ESV). How can you lead a life of love? How can you view the situation differently? How can you trust in God today instead of yourself? Discuss with the group some other strategies to help change their perspectives.

Question 6: Read Galatians 5:22. You can accomplish each spiritual fruit when you give it enough time to ripen. Share with the group one of the fruits of the Spirit you are struggling with. Which one will you work on before the next time you meet?

Question 7: Open your Bibles and read the whole story of Abigail. How does she handle the situation with grace and wisdom? What can you learn from her? How can you be a Christ-fragrance to the world?

Chapter 8: Escape the Bondage of Living for People's Expectations

Question 1: Read Galatians 1:10. When was the last time you did something for only the audience of God? It's toxic and addictive to live for other's approval. Are you living for people's approval, or to love and honour God? Discuss with the group an example of when this has happened to you. Maybe you're in the midst of this struggle right now. If you are, share with the group and allow some time for prayer.

Question 2: One of the keys to living is that we don't have to please God, because we already have Him. We don't have to win His love or attention, because He gives it away freely with no limits—only grace, mercy, discipline, and eternal life. Where do you seek love and attention? Are you a prisoner to people? How can you turn to God's love and mercy? Share openly with the group.

Question 3: Go back to this chapter and read the list of what it's like when we're addicted to approval. Next, read aloud the list describing people who are free from the bondage. What does this tell you?

Question 4: People are meant for good. People are not the enemy, but how we view them can become the enemy. How does God view people? Make a list with the group.

Question 5: Read Matthew 6:24. Discuss with the group how we stop serving two masters.

Question 6: Living for others can become something called self-glory. What does self-glory mean? Where in your life have you stood on your own stage and felt it shaking? How do we turn from self-glory back to only serving God?

Question 7: Read 1 Thessalonians 4:11–12. Why it is important to live a quiet life? What is God saying to you in this passage? How do we live for the audience of the One?

Question 8: I challenge everyone to go on a date with themselves this week. Clear an evening to spend time doing what you want and need to do…whether it's watching your favourite movie, going for a hike, or simply reading a book. You deserve to take care of yourself.

Chapter 9: What Are You Passionate About?

Question 1: What are your passions, dreams, and desires? Write down everything that's going through your mind on a piece of paper. Share with the group. Later, take that piece of paper home and put it somewhere you can read it. A powerful thing happens when we write our goals down on paper.

Question 2: What is your story? I shared my journey of overcoming my learning disability. What impossibilities are holding you back from living out your passion? Read Matthew 19:26 and remember that all things are possible with Christ.

Question 3: Take some time to write out goals, talents, and gifts you have. Then take some time to tell everyone in your group what talents and abilities you think they possess. Many people aren't even aware of the fact that they have a talent and ability within them. Speak life into them today.

Question 4: How do you identify with Queen Esther and her impossible situation? Refer back to the chapter. How do we become fearless in Christ?

Question 5: Discuss with the group why we cannot do everything in our own strength. How do you look to God to strengthen you?

Next, read Ephesians 3:20 and 1 Timothy 4:12. How does this inspire you to live out your God-sized dreams?

Question 6: There are so many people out there who are afraid to live out their dreams and passions. You have the power to help someone accomplish their goals. Make it a priority to do that this week. Next, put all your lists of dreams, goals, and talents into the middle of the circle. Gather around and pray about your passions and dreams. Something amazing happens when we come together and ask God to be a part of our dreams.

Question 7: What does faith and obedience have to do with following our dreams, goals, and passions? How do we remain faithful to God?

Question 8: Why is failure never the end? Share with the group your own experience of failure and how you dealt with it.

Question 9: What does it mean to be a woman seeking God's calling? Would you be okay laying down your dreams and passions to go after God's calling in your life?

Chapter 10: Refuse to Conform to the Patterns of This World

Question 1: Read Romans 12:2. What does it mean to you to refuse to conform to the patterns of this world?

Question 2: What areas or situations in your life do you feel both the world and God are pulling for your attention? Discuss how you could overcome those obstacles. Could it be that our fast-consuming lifestyle is making us care so much about our own well-being and our own fame that we're missing out on God's purpose for us? Discuss with the group.

Question 3: The question we have to ask ourselves is not what we can do for the world, but what does God want us to do for His world. Will you conquer the world, or will you let the world conquer you? Think about that question quietly to yourself. Share with the group if you would like.

Question 4: There is a spiritual battle going on inside of us. Do you feel it? What does it mean to be at war in this way? What does it mean to be in the "battlefield" in the world? How is Satan taking your focus off living for Christ? In what areas must you change? Discuss openly with the group. Remember this is a safe place of trust.

Question 5: In this chapter, you read in Genesis 1 how God created the universe. Isn't God amazing? How can you see the world through God's eyes?

Question 6: Life is a test, life is a trust, and life is a temporary assignment. Read 2 Corinthians 4:18 and discuss with the group.

Question 7: Read Isaiah 55:8–9 and Isaiah 40:31. Everything happens in God's timing, and He holds all the puzzle pieces in place. Leave today knowing God holds the whole world in His hands and He's going to unfold a glorious road for you. I know the greatest adventure lies just ahead.

Chapter 11: Love, Boys, and God

Question 1: Read John 3:16 and 1 Corinthians 13. Why is love so important? How is God the Author of love? Why is it important to love God and yourself before boys come into the picture? Share your views openly.

Question 2: Boys are everywhere. As girls, we are always looking out for our future husbands. Have some fun today as everyone writes out a list of what they require in a potential husband. Share with the group, but most importantly bring that list home with you. It's important to never settle.

Question 3: Read 2 Corinthians 6:14. What does it mean to be unequally yoked? Have you ever thought about this before? Discuss openly with the group what this means to you.

Question 4: Why is it important to be friends first? What happens when we lay that foundation of friendship?

Question 5: Purity affects all areas of one's life. Purity is a life-long goal and entails resisting all temptations and lusts of this world to choose God instead. Refer back to the chapter on my illustration of the word purity. Today, make your own definition of purity. You can either share with the group or keep it to yourself.

Question 6: Jesus is the one who fills our cup. Everything else is just an overflow of that grace. What does this mean? How does Jesus fill your cup?

Question 7: As girls, we need to start praying for our husbands today. Even if we haven't met him, he's out there going through the same impossibilities we are. Take some time to pray openly for him today.

Question 8: Does anyone in the group have more advice on love, boys, dating, and marriage? Share openly with the group, remembering that we can all learn from each other.

Question 9: Take some time to pray for your own purity. Pray for one another today.

Chapter 12: What Is Your Story?

Question 1: We all have a story that's different than anyone else's. It may seem insignificant to you, but it can help direct someone towards the love of Christ. There is only one you, and I think that's pretty amazing. Share with the group part of your testimony. You need all the practice you can get.

Question 2: It's important to have a testimony that is shorter than three minutes. Take some quiet time to prepare this. Refer back to chapter ten on the steps to do this.

Question 3: The best kind of testimony is to become a servant. Read John 15. Discuss with the group how you plan to become a servant today.

Question 4: We don't just have to speak words for it to be a testimony; our actions tell our story as well. How can you put your testimony into your day-to-day actions? Discuss with the group.

Question 5: Even though we're the ones telling the story, God's Holy Spirit is the one working on their heart and mind. You simply plant the seed. Discuss with the group a time when you shared the love of God and they refused to believe. How hard was that for you? Was there a time where you had to wait for them to respond?

Question 6: It's important to become a mentor. You may think you're unqualified, but God can use anyone to help build His kingdom. Who can you start to walk alongside to train them up to be like Christ? Refer back to chapter ten on how you can start doing this.

Question 7: Read Ephesians 4:15. Why is it important to tell our story with love and sensitivity? How do we do this? Always remember it's a privilege to be a part of God's grand masterpiece.

Chapter 13: Run the Race Heavenward

Question 1: Read Philippians 3:20. What does it mean to be a citizen in heaven? How do we live with eternity in mind?

Question 2: Everything was made for God's glory. How do we bring God glory? How can we love God above ourselves?

Question 3: Read Philippians 3:17. Everything will fade away—all our possessions, all our fame, all our money, and all our careers. Life is good, but eternal life is better. What does it mean to live in light of eternity? How can you start living in light of eternity today?

Question 4: Read 1 Corinthians 9:24–25 and 2 Peter 1:10–11. We are all in a marathon, and we won't be finished until we enter the gates of heaven. Oh, what a glorious day that will be! God is going to give each one of us a grand entrance. Can you just imagine what it will be like to see Him face to face? You aren't meant to live on the sidelines. Get up and run the race.

Question 5: Read Psalm 90:12. Why is it important to number our days? Read Ephesians 5:15–17.

Question 6: Read Luke 15:1–7. You and I have the truth. What you are going to do about it? Will you bring the lost sheep home, or will you let them wander forever?

Question 7: Read Habakkuk 2:3. Why is God concerned about you gradually growing? Read 1 Corinthians 2:9 and Psalm 63. Reflect on what God has taught you through His Word and through this book.

Question 8: Together we can be the change. How will you start today?

After reading this book, how has the meaning of beauty changed for you? If you have a story to share or a testimony of how you are embracing your inner beauty and achieving all God has for you, I'd love to hear from you. Feel free to contact me with any questions or your personal testimonial. I hope and pray you live on as a woman who knows she is loved and cherished by the one true King, and never stop until you reach the gates of heaven. I will meet you there.

helpful resources

Dove, G. (2005). *Secrets about Guys that Shouldn't be Secret*. Cincinnati, OH: Empowered Youth Products.

Calhoun, A. A. (2005). *Spiritual Disciplines Handbook: Practices that Transform us*. Downers Grove, IL: Formatio.

Clinton, M. (2010). *Smart Girls, Smart Choices*. Eugene, OR: Harvest House Publishers.

Farrel, P. (2002). *The 10 Best Decisions a Woman Can Make*. Eugene, OR: Harvest House Publishers.

Jaynes, S. (2007). *The Power of a Woman's Words*. Eugene, OR: Harvest House Publishers.

Ludy, E., & Ludy, L. (2009). *When God Writes your Love Story: The Ultimate Guide to Guy/Girl Relationships*. Colorado Springs, CO: Mulynomah Books.

Dr. Townsend, J. (2010). *Now What do I do? The Surprising Solution When Things Go Wrong*. Grand Rapids, MI: Zondervan.

endnotes

1. "Inspiring Quotes from 100 Extraordinary Women," The Huffington Post, accessed February 7, 2017, http://www.huffingtonpost.com/samantha-ettus/100-quotes-from-100-extraordinary-women_b_6483622.html.

2. Rick Warren, *The Purpose Driven Life: What on Earth Am I Here for?* (Grand Rapids: Zondervan, 2002), 254.

3. "Kari Jobe Quotes," AZ Quotes, accessed February 7, 2017, http://www.azquotes.com/quote/1305224.

4. "Audrey Hepburn Quotes," BrainyQuote, accessed February 7, 2017, https://www.brainyquote.com/quotes/quotes/a/audreyhepb394440.html.

5. Lysa TerKeurst, *What Happens When Young Women Say Yes to God: Embracing God's Amazing Adventure for You* (Eugene, Oregon: Harvest House Publishers, 2013), back cover.

6. Rick Warren, *The Purpose Driven Life: What on Earth Am I Here for?* (Grand Rapids: Zondervan, 2002), 204–208.

7. "Quotes of the Day," Time, accessed February 7, 2017, http://content.time.com/time/quotes/0,26174,1597948,00.html.

8. Lysa TerKeurst, *What Happens When Young Women Say Yes to God: Embracing God's Amazing Adventure for You* (Eugene, Oregon: Harvest House Publishers, 2013), 166.

9. "Marilyn Munroe Quotable Quote," Goodreads, accessed February 7, 2017, http://www.goodreads.com/quotes/524215-to-all-the-girls-that-think-you-re-fat-because-you-re.

10. "Candace Cameron Bure Quotable Quote," Goodreads, accessed February 7, 2017, http://www.goodreads.com/quotes/416246-god-created-each-one-of-us-in-our-own-unique.

11. "Lysa TerKeurst Quotable Quote," Goodreads, accessed February 7, 2017, http://www.goodreads.com/quotes/639451-feelings-are-indicators-not-dictators-they-can-indicate-where-your.

12. "Beth Moore, Quotes," Goodreads, accessed February 13, 2017, https://www.goodreads.com/author/quotes/10418.Beth_Moore.

13. Lorna Vanderhaeghe, *A Smart Woman's Guide to Weight Loss* (U.K.: Headline Promotions, Ltd., 2015), 81.

14. "Carrie Underwood Quotable Quote," Goodreads, accessed February 7, 2017, http://www.goodreads.com/quotes/326229-you-can-do-anything-you-put-your-mind-to-i.

15. Shannon Ethridge, *Completely His: Loving Jesus without Limits* (Colorado Springs: WaterBrook Press, 2007), 160–161.

16. Patrick Williams and Diane S. Menendez, *Becoming a Professional Life Coach: Lessons from the Institute for Life Coach Training* (New York: W.W. Norton & Company, 2015), 133.

17. "15 Powerful Quotes from I Am Malala," Move Me Quotes & More, accessed February 7, 2017, http://www.movemequotes.com/i-am-malala/.

18. John Piper, *Don't Waste Your Life* (Wheaton, IL: Crossway, 2009), 81.

19. "Spiritual Dejection," My Utmost for His Highest, accessed February 7, 2017, http://utmost.org.

20. "Love Is … With Rebecca St. James," The Christian Post, accessed February 7, 2017, http://www.christianpost.com/news/love-is-with-rebecca-st-james-48911/.

21. "Candace Cameron Bure Quotable Quote," Goodreads, accessed February 7, 2017, http://www.goodreads.com/quotes/416248-there-will-never-be-another-woman-who-owns-the-look.

22. From the Amy Grant CD *Somewhere Down the Road* (2010), backcover.

23. Rick Warren, *The Purpose Driven Life: What on Earth Am I Here for?* (Grand Rapids: Zondervan, 2002), 40.

works cited

Ethridge, Shannon. *Completely His.* Colorado Springs: Waterbrook Press, 2007.

Piper, J. *Don't Waste Your Life.* Wheaton, IL: Crossway, 2009.

TerKeurst, L. *What Happens When Young Women Say Yes to God.* Eugene, OR: Harvest House Publishers, 2013.

Vanderhaegh, L.R. *A Smart Woman's Guide to Weight Loss.* U.K. Headline Promotions Ltd., 2015.

Warren, R. *The Purpose Driven Life: What on Earth Am I Here For?* Grand Rapids, MI: Zondervan, 2002.

Williams, P. and Menendez, D. *Becoming a Professional Life Coach: Lessons from the Institute for Life Coach Training.* New York: W.W. Norton & Company, 2015.

about
SARAH EVANGELINE

HEY! I'M SARAH. MY FAVOURITE THINGS ABOUT THIS LIFE ARE PEOPLE, ice cream, music, and exploring God's creation. He has taken me on an amazing adventure I call faith. God is our firm foundation, and we must all live to honour and glorify Him the best way we can. My greatest passion is inspiring young women to embrace their inner beauty and find their identity in Christ.

I'm a graduate of Liberty University with a degree in psychology and counselling. I am currently studying for my Master's in Human Services Counselling: Life Coaching. I am a proud Canadian, but I also plan on travelling to each end of the globe. My family and friends are my pride and joy. My hobbies are travelling, photography, and baking. I will live the rest of my days for the Lord, wherever He may take me.

I absolutely love writing. Writing allows me to release what's going on inside my mind. When I put my words onto paper, I learn so much about myself and God. Sometimes God wakes me up at 5:00 a.m. just to show me what I'm to write. I hope my words can inspire, encourage, challenge, and help others learn more about life and our amazing Creator.

Website: http://sburford5.wix.com/sarahevangeline

Sarah63journeyon

Sarah Evangeline

Email: Sarah would love to hear feedback on how this book impacted your life. She also loves hearing testimonies and your own words of wisdom.

Sarah63Evangeline@gmail.com

Check out Sarah's blog:
Simple Joys

JOY. IT'S MY FAVOURITE WORD. IT'S MY FAVOURITE THING. AND I WANT to share it with you.

For most of my life, I never really truly understood it. I never valued it. I never truly experienced what it was like to have that true joy and what it can do for someone's life. You know … that joy that grows deep in your soul and touches every aspect of your life? It's the kind of joy only Jesus Christ, my Lord and Saviour, can give. I used to settle for temporary happiness. I was okay with being the "good enough" Christian. But I have learned along this amazing adventure I call faith that I must seek after this abundance of joy and grace.

I want you to stop settling for worldly happiness and experience pure joy. Abundance joy. Everlasting joy. Simple joy. 'Cause I have found that it's in the simple, tiny, still moments that the greatest treasures are found. Yes, you and I will still have our bad days from time to time. We'll still experience feelings of doubt and regret. We'll still have trials and pain. But my prayer and hope is that you make every day a day to set out and find God's joy and experience it so you can touch someone else's life too.

You won't find joy in the big and shiny materialistic values of the world. You won't find it on the cover of a magazine or on your favourite TV show. You won't get it from pretending to be "perfect." You'll find joy by answering to the still, small voice of God. He gives this strength of joy away freely, but we must seek it out and cherish it. I have written these simple joy scripts as a reminder of why we keep on keeping on. These are reminders of faith and how God can use every single broken piece in our lives for His glory.

You are so worth loving every piece of your life and what God can do in it! Every single day, God is trying to reach out to you, to give you His joy. This life is all about Him. And when we finally realize that, the first simple joy is born.

Join me on this journey,
Sarah

http://sburford5.wixsite.com/sarahevangeline

meet the girls

WE ALL HAVE A STORY TO TELL. EVERYONE'S STORY COUNTS AND IS needed in this world. This book is not just about me, but about every single girl in this world who wants to embrace everything that God has for them. I am so unbelievably thankful for the group of ladies who helped bring this book to life. Each one of them has become a personal friend of mine, and has encouraged me in my own walk with God. I hope you all were blessed by their testimony.

Kelly Zuidema

Hi, I'm Kelly. I have had a love for writing for most of my life. I have graduated with a distinction from Booth University College with a Bachelor's Degree in Religious Studies. I am currently a child and youth pastor in Winnipeg's multi-cultural inner city, where I am living out my biblical calling to bring hope to the nations and empower girls to see themselves through the eyes of Jesus.

Rebecca Reimer

I'm Rebecca and I'm 24 years old. I am married to the love of my life, Trevor and we have two beautiful children, Xavier and Alexa. I am an extrovert, so I like to keep busy and be out with other people. I am currently the publisher of a sports magazine and I teach piano. I also enjoy playing the piano and singing in our church praise team. On the outside it might look like I am doing it all, but I am always trying to find a balance between my family, work and God. I've chosen this life because it takes a lot of prayer and hard work. No one is perfect, and we're all just trying to do our best. I pray this book helps you to grow and become the woman God intended you to be!

Cassie Barrett

My name is Cassie Barrett. I am 20 years old and I grew up in St. Thomas, Ontario. I'm currently studying Medical Radiation Sciences at McMaster University. I have had many ups and downs in my faith journey. I have asked many difficult questions and had my fair share of doubts, but I truly know that God has worked in great ways in my life through difficult situations. Part of my story is in this book. I hope and pray that this book will be an encouragement to many.

Kathryn Gross

My name is Kathryn, but everyone calls me Kat. I love the colour green, going camping, eating good food, playing guitar, and worshipping God. The older I get the more I realize that God should always be our number one interest. It wasn't always easy to see Him at times in my life. It was easier for me to deny Him instead of facing my sins head on. I thank God every day for changing me into the beautiful woman I am and showing me how amazing life is when I follow His plans for me. Never doubt in the dark, what God told you in the light.

Jordan Robinson

My name is Jordan Robinson. I have recently moved to Saint Thomas, Ontario to study at Fanshawe College for Child and Youth Care. When I first moved to St. Thomas, it was a struggle. Becoming independent is not an overnight change, but it has defiantly grown and shaped me. I have felt loneliness and despair, but I am thankful for my church family, and all the amazing people around me. When we think about what could be next in our life, it can be nerve-racking and scary, but I want to encourage you all to put your full trust in God because He has perfect timing for you and He holds your future. Just remember that God is always good, He has placed you where you are for a reason, but don't be afraid to open your eyes to the amazing opportunities He has in store for you ahead!

Rebekah McNeilly

Hey I'm Rebekah! I am in third year university at McMaster in Hamilton, Ontario. I have an adventurous side to climb those big waterfalls, but I also want to seek out God in those still, small moments. This is a big, big world and I am so glad I know God as my personal Saviour. I do not know what is up ahead, but I do know that by trusting in Him, it will be beyond my wildest dreams.

Emily Sears

My name is Emily Sears and I am a lover of Jesus Christ. My parents are pastors of the Salvation Army church, which is the main reason why I have grown into the relationship I have with the Lord today. I am twenty-one, studying to be a Social

Service Worker, and have two part time jobs. I work at a retirement home, and I also have the amazing opportunity to work as a Support Worker for an autistic teenaged girl. An exciting thing is happening in my life right now is that I am engaged to a godly young man and we will be getting married in January, 2018! God is good, and I am very excited for where He is taking me.

Annalee Olthof

Hello. I'm Annalee. I have been friends with Sarah since our teen years and we recently became next door neighbours. Our friendship has continued to grow and strengthen over the years. I am a wife to my wonderful husband, Joshua and a mama to our son, Markus. I pray this book encourages you as you learn and grow more in the love of our Savior.

Corisa Miller

Hi, I am Corisa. I am an early childhood educator and have a passion for working with children, youth, woman and the LGBT community as a whole. I am a child of God and I want to live radically for Him. I believe that we are called to love authentically. I am a dreamer and idealist. I can be a perfectionist, but I am learning to "embrace the mess". I am no longer letting "the mess" in my life define me, but I am being bold in my faith and letting God use my mess for His glory. I hope you all can do the same!

Lisa Campbell
(Lisa.Campbell.Photography)

Hi, I'm Lisa! I was born in Chatham-Kent, Ontario, a small city located between London and Windsor. Attending our local Christian school is where Sarah and I became friends 17 years ago. We have seen each other through most of elementary school, high school, and - though many kilometers a part at times - college and university. In college I learned the skills and techniques to support, enrich, and grow my fondness of photography and to create my own brand. Assisting Sarah with some digital aspects of this project has been a delight. Her perseverance and dedication to this work is a testament to her consistent approach in life. Most recently, Sarah and I traveled to Israel together where we were baptized in the Jordan River. It was an impactful moment for me, enhanced by the presence and shared experience of a cherished friend. Sarah, I applaud you on this exceptional achievement and wish you abundant success in all you aspire to do.